Clowns and Capers
Some True Stories of a Private Eye

BY

Russ Bubas

"Dedicated to my two beautiful daughters, Tracey and Holly, who managed to laugh more with me than at me."
       - Russ Bubas

Copyright © 2011 by Russ Bubas
Library of Congress Control Number 978-1461113072
ISBN 1461113075

All rights reserved. No part of this book may be reproduced or transmitted in any form or by any means, electronic or mechanical, including photocopying, recording, or by any information storage and retrieval system, without permissions in writing from the copyright owner.

This book was printed in the United States of America

To order additional copes of this book, contact:
Zingology Press
www.zingologypress.com
info@zingology.com

PREFACE

Many years ago, with the energy, zeal and stupidity of youth, and with a bit of serendipity, I started paying my way through NYU by working with a private detective agency. The owner was a genuine New York character, and still, after forty some years, one of the most amazing guys I've ever run across. He spotted things I never did, never ceased to amaze me with his sharp eye, and hardly ever slept. A walking film noir.

    As a green college kid, I had no idea what I wanted to do in life and was taking things a day (and party) at a time. My boss, the owner of the agency, Erwin, was slightly pear shaped with Jack Nicolson eyebrows. He would pick me up after class and we would roam the city like minor avenging angels, staking out grocery stores to look for employees stealing food, make purchases at hot dog stands and bars to detecting servers clipping sales and tail delivery trucks to see if anything fell out the back the truck. We would range up and down the Jersey Turnpike and New York Thruway and into the shady bowels of Queens and Brooklyn and the Bronx. Being from a small town upstate, the City was an exciting and totally diverse universe. Every day was an adventure, every night exciting.

Erwin as a businessman was two or three clicks below Forest Gump. He had virtually no outside interests; never went to the movies, never read any books. He did his PI work eighteen to twenty hours a day, seven days a week. I realized why; he had so much fun.

I stayed a good while with Erwin, and did four years as a counterintelligence officer. I tried another agency, did a stint in retail loss prevention, and eventually went out on my own. The vast majority of work that I, and later, my agency of some thirty people did, were corporate investigations, detecting employee dishonesty, substance abuse, inefficiency and even industrial espionage. I've learned the art of interrogation, deductive reasoning and following clues and hunches. My files have literally thousands of signed confessions. I've gone into court to prosecute people, testified at union and labor relations hearings and gotten back hundreds of thousands of dollars in restitution for my clients.

None of that makes as good cocktail party patter as the few domestic cases I've worked. Corporate criminals, for the most part, are motivated by greed, stupidity and sometimes revenge. Interesting only if there is some twist to their nefarious deeds or their level of theft is so high it gets your attention. On the other had, human interactions with each other often make no sense at all and are usually head shaking amusing.

I've put together some cases, out of many, that easily come to mind. In these, the unexpected becomes the norm, no two days are alike. and they provide curious insight into human folly. There are many more like these.

While I never made a lot of money, I loved every minute of it, and wouldn't change much at all. It's a lucky guy who has enjoyed his work as much as I have. I plan, like Erwin, never to give it up.

Contents

Getting My Feet Wet...1

A Lot of Bad Guys Out There...7

Learning the Hard Way..15

Things Are Not Always What They Seem....................21

Serial Liars..31

Never Give Up...53

Lucky and Good..61

Being a PI Can Be Pretty Sleazy.......................................69

He Did Two Things Well..81

Married People Are Crazy..111

Trouble on the Mountain...121

Sorry I Did It, Even Once..139

GETTING MY FEET WET
Life is full of serendipity

"Here's the plan," Erwin said. His sly smile drawing a line under his arched eyebrows let me know that this was going to be a different kind of plan. I'd been working with Erwin for about three weeks and was, frankly, having the time of my life. He was New York slick, never seemed to sleep and bombed around the city in a Chevy convertible I dubbed "the detection tank". My goal was to try to earn enough money to get me through NYU and Erwin would let me work as much as I wanted. I was rapidly becoming a sidekick in his 20 hour days.

"We're going to crawl on the inside of the ceiling and I'm going to take a movie of her clipping sales. The maintenance guy has already moved the ceiling panel right above that cash register. We're going to get her good!" He said, grinning.

"Huh?"

The issue, as Erwin explained earlier, was a grandmotherly-like cashier with 16 years seniority, who was suspected of not ringing up customer sales and tossing the money she was collecting into her purse, hidden under the counter. This nefarious criminal was working in an employee cafeteria in a giant office building on Sixth Avenue, and, as she only worked the lunch hour, was a busy little thief.

This being the early seventies, Erwin's camera was the size and weight of a violin case filled with cinder blocks. Erwin himself had a low center of gravity. He was as light weight as a Mini Cooper. The struts holding up the ceiling were as thin as fettuccini. His plan had us crawling the length of a football field on the ceiling struts, towing his Cecile B. DeMille movie camera behind him, while three thousand Manhattan worker bees clambered below in luncheon chaos. I had grave doubts about this plan.

"You know, it might be better if we both didn't go;" I said, hoping to sound confident while trying to hide my abject fear. "Maybe I can buy something and if she steals it, you can get me paying her." I set my jaw.

He pondered for a minute. It was 11:50 and already the cafeteria was filling up.

"Good idea", he exclaimed. You get something and pay her the exact amount. Mark the bills like I showed you. We'll get her coming and going." He was getting that adrenalin rush I'd come to recognize when he was getting close to catching someone,

I exhaled slowly and silently.

"OK, it will take about ten minutes or so to get to her spot. I'll start filming right away and you get some food and get in her line. I'll keep shooting. Then come back here and we'll go in together and take her off the job." Erwin was ready to go. He gave me a mongoose-like smile.

In a back room was a steel rung ladder, disappearing up to the inside of the ceiling. Out in the cafeteria, the din of clanking dishes and rushing and munching secretaries was rapidly growing louder. I figured I could buy a hamburger, pay the suspect with my marked bills, and then eat it on the run. I'd be out of there and back within minutes, waiting for Erwin's next move. This was better than TV. With some final and confusing instructions, that I didn't understand, Erwin started up the ladder, surprisingly nimble. I watched his fruit basket butt disappear above the ceiling and his camera bang against the ladder rungs as he pulled it up by the strap.

By now, the luncheon cafeteria was in full riot condition. People at the hot foods and the salad bar wandered around, trays in hands, looking for a table that wasn't populated by hostiles. Luscious young women were chattering like chipmunks on amphetamines.

There were three checkout counters. Discreetly looking up, I found the ceiling tile with a three inch opening on its side. Immediately below, merrily punching in numbers on her cash register was a grandmotherly lady, soft as a pillow; the suspect. She didn't look like a career criminal, but, just out of my teens, what did I know?

There were lines everywhere and I had to push my way around to grab a tray and a hamburger and get into position for Erwin's camera evidence collection. I made it into line at the check out counter and was shuffling behind a young and attractive woman wearing a bulging silk blouse and nicely stuffed skirt, and who was pushing her tray along with a large bowl of Minestrone soup on it. I tried not to look up at the ceiling where this probably insane private eye was creeping, so I concentrated on her cute bottom.

Unknown to me, or about two thousand dazed office workers, Erwin had somehow made it across the inside of the ceiling without serious incident and, at the same time, was actually looking down at the cashier from the darkness above. Then, a mistake: He decided to get a little more comfortable and moved onto his side. As he shifted, he placed the camera down. As the ceiling tile was canted, the camera starting sliding down towards the opening. He desperately grabbed for it.

"Aaaargh!!" He cried, as the tile let go and he dropped from the ceiling, upside down, like an inverted turtle. He made a messy turtle three point landing in the bowl of Minestrone. It was like a safe, dressed in a suit, fell out of the sky.

Screams were everywhere. The good looking babe in front of me now wore most of her soup on her white blouse and was hyperventilating and on the verge of hysteria. Everyone nearby was jumping around yelling and pointing at the body that had dropped from the ceiling like two hundred pounds of wet pancakes. I stood there stunned.

Erwin, however, quick as a cat, jumped up, shook himself, and reached his paw over, grabbing the cashier by her wrist and yelling, "Gotcha."

The cashier totally intimidated and terrified by this aerial attack, immediately confessed, crying out, "I'm sorry I stole," then broke into tears. Erwin, now standing dripping in Minestrone soup, as if everything was planned, told her to follow him off the floor to the office where she then wrote out a complete statement of her years of embezzlement, promising never to steal again.

Not knowing what else to do, I left my hamburger

on the counter and followed with my best game face. The manager stood ashen-faced just outside the office as we marched in with the culprit.

As Erwin walked her in, the manager exclaimed to me, "God, he takes his job seriously, doesn't he? I never though he would jump out of the ceiling to catch her."

I realized he was totally awe struck with me as a member of this Batman style incident. I was still stunned by what Erwin did, but gathered myself with my new found status.

"When he sees bad things happening, sometimes Erwin gets so angry, he can't control himself," I lied, making like a mini super hero.

"Wow, you guys are something." He said, impressed.

"Yeah, we are." I replied a little smugly.

I knew then I was going to love this job. That was some forty years ago. I learned everything I could from Erwin, who never ceased to amaze me. We climbed trees to peer into windows, followed trucks for days, and checked more bars and restaurants than I can remember. I stayed with him throughout college and beyond. I beefed up my experience with a four year stint in Military Intelligence as a Counterintelligence Officer, running a field office in Buffalo, then investigations in Korea. They taught me how to pick locks (never used it), tail people (used that a lot), burn papers without leaving an ash (used it once) and other tricks of the trade.

Coming back to the states, I went back with Erwin for a while, then did some retail loss prevention and then locates and investigations with another agency in Boston. Then I opened my own agency.

Never forgetting the times running around the City with Erwin, I somehow managed to keep my sense of adventure, not to mention my sense of humor. Over the years, there have been so many stories, and misadventures, that many have been forgotten. Here are a few of the ones that remain remembered, mostly with a smile.

A LOT OF BAD GUYS OUT THERE
Guys, who talk tough, usually are not.

I had a client (and sort-of friend) who had a non-stop and fervent taste for women. There were many and all were stunning. One of the more serious ones, and probably the best, was Michelle, a tall, striking blonde, a model, actress, and former wife of a major league ballplayer. She made your face go numb. My client (I'll call him John) hungered for her like Caesar for Gaul.

The problem was that she was already involved with an annoying mobster wannabe, Tony. Tony was a flash around town, making grand entrances into the restaurants du jour, leaving his Mercedes convertible in front so all could watch him usher her in, trying not to step on his tongue while doing so. Tony would flex his muscles whenever he could, bragged like a high school quarterback, and liked nothing better to imply he was connected. Not Mister T., but he had a strong affection for gold hanging on his chest which would glitter down the length of any bar, attracting females like fish to lures. Michelle, who could turn the head of a coma patient, made a wonderful accessory for him. Tony made it clear to whom she belonged.

But John had a good shot, as Michelle was trying to get out of this relationship, and John had the advantage of some real money. Tony was not in tune with her idea, and certainly didn't like losing. In fact he thought he and Michelle should live happily ever after and was not about to let her jump on someone else. This difference of opinion escalated to a point where Michelle was scared to death of Tony, who, when not trying to pick up waitresses, was stalking and clinging to her like a bad rash. A restraining order did little good. Changing her phone number didn't work either. Tony was relentless in professing his undying love. God help her if she didn't reciprocate.

John told her he would come to her rescue, knowing full well his chances of hot monkey sex would seriously escalate if he did. Of course, John wanted nothing to do with Tony. So he called me.

I chatted with Michelle and found her concerns were credible. Tony was way beyond a scorned lover, he was a serious stalker and the threats, although veiled, were decidedly unsettling. He was a troubling character and the friction between them was palatable.

But, he was slowly backing off like a dangerous bear tiring of his prey. A bone of contention was the jewelry he had given her over time. During their steamy affair, whenever they went anywhere, Tony would treat her with a bobble of some kind. The trip to The Bahamas warranted an emerald broach. The weekend in New York won a very pretty diamond bracelet, and so on. Tony finally said he would go away, but he wanted all of his jewelry gifts back. Michelle had no problem returning everything, but didn't want to go anywhere near him. Scared to death. Maybe this was something I could help her with, being the go-between.

So one bright summer morning, I drove over to Michelle's garden condo and found her sunbathing in back in her Frenchiest bikini. Tucking herself in and with the same smile that I'm sure devastated Tony, not to mention John, she led me inside and offered a glass of wine. As it was ten in the morning, I passed on that and asked to see the gifts Tony had bestowed on her. When she showed me, I was stunned. I understood perfectly why Tony and all were interested in her. Aside from being beautiful, she must be very, very good. In a paper bag, there was some thirty pieces: rings, necklaces, bracelets, all gorgeous.

I made of list of them; describing the best I could and then accepted that wine. She poured from a cold bottle bearing a French label. Michelle's life was very interesting. Aside from modeling, she even did a short stint as a TV talk show hostess. The legends of the parties she had while married to a major league pitcher were a window into his declining career. But, she was more than eye candy; a lot more. Here was a woman with a sense of humor, smart and with a zest for life, not to mention a body that exuded sensuality. I would've helped her free of charge.

At that time, I had a guy working for me that could qualify as a character from a Spenser novel. Hector was part Mashpee Indian, part Afro-American and all scary. He was six foot, six and weighed in around 280. Bald head and a loping gait. Once a rookie police officer, he was in the wrong place at the wrong time and was dismissed from the force. He came in looking for "I can do anything" kind of job. I hired him on the spot.

I decided that Hector was the best courier I could find for this little job and he was eager to go. You got the feeling Hector ate tough guys for lunch. So, I did what was the smart thing; took my bag of jewels to the jewelry building where I had a friend. I asked him for a formal appraisal on all the pieces, with valid descriptions, rather than my Mickey Mouse inventory. He called me two days later.

"Dan, guess what? The stuff you left off for me to appraise; well, it's all junk." He said. I could hear him chuckling on the phone.

"What? What do you mean all junk?"

"Just what I said. It's all fake. The most valuable piece is worth about a hundred bucks." He said.

Great. Now I knew why Tony was so anxious t get they jewelry back. If the word got out that he was giving out fake stuff to his honey, and pretending it was real, his reputation would fall apart. Tony the big spender would suddenly become Tony the phony.

"OK, please give me accurate descriptions and list the estimated value of each. I appreciate it." I said. I figured Hector would have fun with this.

He came into the office silently, considering his size. Hector had the grace of a natural athlete, and the smile of a predator. I showed him the inventory list that itemized each piece, described it and listed its approximate value. He grinned at me.

"Take this list and the jewelry over to Atlantic Avenue and see our "friend" Tony Tremonte there. I need you to show him each piece, and have him sign after its description on the inventory sheet. Once he's looked at it all and signed for it, give it to him and thank him politely. "Bring the signed sheet back to me," I instructed.

"When do you want me to see him?"

"He shows up pretty much on schedule, and God knows what he does there. He flies around at night like a bat, so I would say tomorrow after 11 or so, should be good."

"Will he give me a hard time?" Hector smiled when he asked.

"Don't know. He thinks he's a tough guy. Be polite, but leave if it looks like it's going to get ugly. No sense having any problems with the guy." Hector smiled wider.

"OK, boss, consider it done".

The next morning, Hector showed up in his normal street attire, a full length black leather trench coat, black leather slacks and black turtle neck, dressed pretty much like a vampire linebacker. All parts, including the nicely shaved top of his head, had a slight sheen. He was like some graceful aquatic animal, stepping out of the sea. He inventoried the jewels again, put it all in a briefcase and took off. A couple strolling by stepped aside and stared as he climbed into his black Cadillac pimpmobile.

The office was a small box, built on a short pier jutting into the marina. There was glass on the water side and a narrow deck on both sides. The street entrance was a plain oak door with a stained brass plaque saying "Mondo Enterprises" There was a hydrant on the street in front where Tony's Mercedes was parked. Hector parked down the street and walked past twice. There was no activity visible. He tried the front door, found it unlocked and walked into an empty reception area, carpeted in dark green shag with pine paneling. On top of the unoccupied reception desk was five days worth of junk mail and an empty wine bottle. Despite the location it did not look like a flourishing business. From the door to the inner office could be heard oldies rock and roll music. Hector pushed it open and walked in like the grim reaper.

Tony had his feet on his desk and was immersed in the latest issue of *Penthouse.*

"What the fuck!" He said when Hector strode in. He pulled his feet off the desk, but remained sitting.

Hector stopped and held his hand up, silencing any further protests. He gave Tony his best predatory grin. "My boss is returning this to you. He says you would know what it is. I need you to sign for it so my boss knows you got it back." He said very quietly, Tony straining to hear.

With that, he put the briefcase on Tony's desk and snapped it open. He took out a single piece, placed in on the desk and scanned the inventory sheet.

"OK, one broach, containing eight small Cubic Zirconia stones in a horseshoe pattern." He placed the sheet down next to the bracelet and pointed to the descriptive line with a pen.

Tony was silent as he stared at the broach. He looked at the receipt, back at the bobble, then up at Hector. His face was the color of flour. Except for his breathing, the room was silent for a moment, then, from the back of his throat, almost imperceptible at first, started a low sobbing. It grew until he was almost hyperventilating.

"You didn't have to do this," He gasped. "I would've let her keep it all, if she wanted."

Hector waited, silent, relaxed. After a minute, he again pointed to the line for signature with his pen. Tony, gasping now, trying to control himself, reached across, took the pen and scribbled his name. This went on for the next twenty minutes as Hector went through the thirty-odd pieces and Tony struggled to not completely break down. He didn't quite make it as his nose filled and his eyes reddened. Tony was crying.

When finished, Hector took the inventory sheet and dropped it and his pen into the now empty case, clicking it closed. He smiled again and started to turn to walk out, then stopped.

"One more thing I was supposed to tell you. Leave Michelle alone. Don't contact her, come near her or even think about her.. It's over." It came out as a whisper, more frightening than a scream.

He then walked back outside and drove his Cadillac back to the office. He came in, draped himself in a chair and opened his coat. I noticed he was carrying.

"Mission accomplished, boss."

"He give you a hard time?"

"Nah, routine."

"Thanks, Hector, put it on your time sheet. Give me call in the morning. Got another little job for you."

"OK, boss. See you tomorrow." With than he gathered himself up and started loping out. He stopped just before the door and turned. "Know what?"

"What?"

"Not so tough"
"Didn't think so." I replied.

LEARNING THE HARD WAY
There is usually a good mistake a day.

Working in New York, young, eager and stupid, in addition to the all night surveillances, I was assigned as a bar spotter. The idea was to go into a bar owned by a client and pose as a regular customer. Being inconspicuous and acting natural, you buy some drinks and watch to make sure the bartender rings up the sales and puts the money in the till, instead of his pocket. Pretty simple.

We learned some sneaky tricks to give a bad guy the opportunity to be up to bad behavior, like buying the first drink with a large bill, and leaving the change on the bar. Later, you tell the bartender to take payment for the succeeding drinks out of the change, giving him the option to "forget" to ring up for the second or third drink. Sometimes, a savvy bartender would not collect until you were leaving, or were out the door. In that way, you couldn't see if the drink was rung up or the money went south. In that case, we would remember a series of sales that were rung up prior to leaving, and the exact time you made the transaction. In that way, the client could search and find where your sale should be on the register journal tape to see if it was properly entered in the register. Our clients ranged from the posh Four Seasons, where they had special coolers for the Russian and Polish vodkas, to the shot and a beer crowd at the Blarney Stone, where you could get a only-in-New York corned beef sandwich and wash it down with shooters of

Wild Turkey.

Of course, the occupational hazard was drinking all the booze you were buying. You had to buy at least two drinks in any place you checked, and some were poured like the Kool Aid dispenser at a cult camp. Often, after three or four audits, you forgot what you were doing, where you were, and even who you were. So, interesting ways of disposing of the booze, other than ingesting it, were invented. Woe to the planted plant that was in arm's reach of the bar. And, if there was a nice thick plush carpet under the stool, it often squished when we walked out.

Trying to be ingenious, I figured out that if I took the rubber bulb from a squirting flower trick, I could use it to suck up the booze from a glass. I practiced. I would palm the rubber bulb, and then put my elbows on the bar with my hands over the glass and point the nozzle down. Of course, I would have to have a shot or at least a drink without ice or mixer. I could then quietly squeeze the bulb, and insert the rubber nipple into the glass, then let it go. Viola! The booze was nicely sucked up into the bulb, just like I had poured it into my already abused body. I could then just put the thing in my pocket to squeeze it out somewhere discreet.

This particular day was a hot August New York scorcher, the air thick with palatable grit and short tempers. Stepping from the street into any bar or pub down near Canal Street took two to three minutes for your eyes to adjust from the white light, to the dark cavern-like inside the dives. As usual, I was assigned a list of seven targets to spot, almost all bars, with a few snack bars mixed in. At least I could get a rubbery hot dog to suck up the booze and keep me going.

I had already checked two bars and had downed four drinks before I headed for a joint near the docks that could have passed for the black hole of Calcutta. This was a down and dirty, back alley type of dive, almost guaranteed to have watered drinks and a thieving bartender mixed in with the scent of sweat and hard luck. I had my pen and paper, tape recorder and drink sucker-upper in place when I walked in, the ready investigator.

There was only one other guy at the bar, a grizzled drunk who looked like he hadn't moved off the bar stool for at least two weeks. His head was drooping dangerously near his finger print covered glass. He was wearing wool so I figured he wasn't very fashion conscious.

The bartender was the size of a cement mixer and about as subtle. I was a skinny kid wearing khakis and a polo shirt. I felt like a cookie on the dessert buffet. I slid onto the stool, three away from the drunk and tried to look casual. Scratching himself, the bartender shuffled over after a minute and stood in front, daring me to order. I ordered a Dewar's, neat, ready to do my magic.

The drink was free poured to the brim of a rocks glass. About five ounces of misery. My liver was sending bad signals to my brain. I figured this was the time for my tricky little booze sucker upper. So, waiting for the bartender to again stare open mouthed at the TV soap opera, I palmed my rubber bulb from my pocket, stuck the end into my glass of scotch and let it go. Quietly, it slurped. Success! But, when I looked down I saw only half was gone. That was OK, I would pretend I'd taken a gulp, and wait for a chance to get the rest. A couple of minutes later, I was ready to again to make my move.

Bridging my hands over the glass, I slyly around and saw no one paying attention to me, the dumb kid down the bar. Cupping the squeegee in my hand, I stuck the nozzle down and squeezed. Forgetting it was already mostly full, warm scotch rushed like a geyser from my rubber bulb nozzle into the glass in a violent stream, gushing into what was remaining at the bottom of the glass and blowing up and out into my face and onto the bar. I was soaked and wide-eyed in terror.

"Holy shit," the drunk yelled, looking over at me in horror. "His drink blew up. Wow!" He was more awake than he'd been in the past month, his eyes suddenly opened as big as lemon slices and his jaw hanging open. He turned back and stared at his drink as if it was creature also poised to attack.

"His drink blew up!" he yelled again, leaning back in fear away from his glass.

"What the fuck is going on?" growled the bartender, reaching underneath for his sapper. He started lumbering down the bar towards me, menace in his eye. The bar in front of me was soaked with scotch, which was also dripping down my face. My shirt had a large wet circle in the middle, and it was dripping off the bar onto my lap. I looked like a finalist in a wet tee shirt contest.

"Nothing", I mumbled. "I just spilled a little."

"Spilled a little! You threw the whole damn

glass all over my bar!"

"Not really. Sorry." I was stricken with fear. I had blown my cover and was stupidly looking around for a rescue. The drunk continued to look at his drink, then mine, obviously wondering if it was an infectious malady. The bartender was wondering if anyone would miss me. Then I saw it in his eyes. He realized I was a spotter, a dumb one at that. A slow grin moved across the stubble in his face. He tossed over a moldy bar rag, chuckling at me like a serial killer.

I gave the bar a fast wipe, threw down some money and quick walked out, apologizing and squishing the whole way. As I passed the drunk he asked what I was drinking, hoping he could up his octane.

My report was very thin and I never told my boss.

THINGS AREN'T ALWAYS WHAT THEY SEEM
People are really, really interesting.

Donald was visibly nervous, shifting around in the visitor's chair like he was sitting on something bad he could catch through his pants.

"I could probably get fired for this," he said in a quiet voice. "But I talked it over with Sheila; she's the bookkeeper, and she agrees something has to be done."

I waited a minute. "So, you both agree to this, and you're doing it for your boss, but without his permission."

He looked beaten down. "That's right, but we think something has to be done."

I was silent for a minute. Donald was an old acquaintance. I had worked for his Dad and knew the family. He was a solid guy. His call had come in earlier, and he asked if he come to the office right away to discuss a problem. He told me he was now the operations director of a small, three unit hotel chain, and it was job related. His nerves vibrated through the phone.

On the early autumn day, a cool wind filtered in from the sea, pushing with it a flagstone fog that settled on the roofs of the higher buildings. Defying the crisp temperature, Don came in with a glisten of sweat that wrinkled his shirt. A usually positive and happy go lucky guy, he looked like he was coming in for gum surgery. He sat down heavily in the director's chair opposite my desk, his face hanging.

I put on my best confessional expression. "How can I help, Don?"

He was quiet for a minute. "I will probably get fired for this, but I've talked it over with the Sheila and she agrees we have to do this." He said again. Don paused, thinking how to begin. Then shrugged.

"About six months ago, the owner, my boss, Boris Hovanisian hired an assistant. I think you know him, Dan. He's been around forever and does pretty well. But he's pushing eighty and I think he's losing it."

I nodded. I knew a little about him and the company. Closely and privately held, the boutique hotels, while small, were positioned in the best locations possible. Old Boris was known for his ugly temper and harsh business practices. Old school and not a great guy to work for.

Don continued, "Well, this assistant is about forty but looks younger. She wears short skirts and flaunts her figure. Sheila swears she doesn't wear underwear, but I wouldn't know. I'm afraid to peek. She's ingratiated herself with Boris to a point where he's given her full access to practically everything including check signing privileges. He lets her stick her nose into all the books and mail. She's even gotten him to open a separate bank account that we aren't supposed to know about. She's the only one with access to it. She is badmouthing us behind our backs to a point where Boris doesn't believe us and only her."

"So, is old Boris jumping on her bones?"

"No doubt," Don paused. "I hate to visualize it. Anyway, we are convinced she is not who she says she is. If you can do a background on her and show she's a phony, maybe Boris will come to his senses and get rid of her."

"Sure, Don, I can do this, but you know it could be risky to you. If she comes up clean, and the word gets out that you did this, lover boy will not think kindly of you."

"I know, Dan. But, she's ruining the company. Sheila thinks she's manipulating the figures and stealing. You've got to do this and do it so no one knows. I'm sure she's not who he thinks she is and it's the only way we can convince him to get her out of things."

I thought for a minute. "OK, Don. What's her name and address? We'll start with previous employments, do an identity check, and look for liens and judgments. I'll be discreet and keep you updated as the information comes in."

"Thanks, Dan." A little color came to his face. "I knew I could count on you."

With that, he reached into his jacket pocket and came out with a folded packet. "It's as much as we have. Her name is Chantal Morgan. Her application has mysteriously disappeared so I wrote down as much as I could remember about what she said when she started."

I shuffled through his notes. Wasn't much there, but enough. "OK, Don. We'll do what we can. Give me a number where I can reach you in private and I'll keep you posted."

He thanked me again and left. I glanced out my window and saw him huddling close to the buildings as he made his way back down Boylston Street. He acted like it was colder than it was.

We started running an identity check through some back door databases. It turned out Ms. Morgan was using a couple of social security numbers, and her original name was Moesky. She moved around a lot and seemed to spend more money than she earned. I found a past employment with a law firm I knew. She only worked there about ten months, but Peter Mantel, a sharp guy who used to be a state rep worked there and was plugged in all over the place. I met him for lunch at the Legal Seafood Bar, next to the

Aquarium. The lunch crowd was a combination of tourists and local business men. You could tell the locals by the drinks they ordered with their chowders. The tourists ordered coke with their lobsters. We each ordered the crab cakes, the best I had since Baltimore. I took a good sized bite and washed it down with my Amstel Light.

"Peter, you remember a babe working for your firm about fours ago? A hottie. Calls herself Chantal Morgan."

Peter's slow grin told me on was onto something good. "This is off the record," He said. Everything with Peter was off the record, as with every pol who ever served the great Commonwealth of Massachusetts. "This is fun. What I hear is Ms Chantal started boffing one of the major partners, who was inconveniently married at the time. Supposedly it was one of the situations where he couldn't get enough. Blow jobs in the elevator; back seat of his Mercedes in the parking lot. Somehow, she got him into phone sex. Classic case of a guy thinking with the wrong head."

"I feel a sexual harassment complaint lurking."

"Better. What I hear was that councilor was talking dirty into her voice mail machine. After she got some really juicy recordings, she got around to asking for "loans" and other assistance. He resisted and she brought out her answering machine, played back his hot little messages and threatened to make complaint and go public with them, which I hear would burn the ears off a street walker. Not only was there a wife, he was the President of the Mass Bar at the time."

"Ouch. I take it he made it go away."

"It went away with some serious go-away money. Don't know how much, but hot little Ms. Morgan supposedly bought herself a new car and condo right after she left."

I took another sip of beer and thought for a second. This sounds like bad news for old Boris. I picked up lunch.

Don took this bit of information with a groan. "God, she's going to screw him in other ways. When he's screwed, we are too."

"So far, she's panning out to be the quintessential conniving bitch," I said. She's got credit all over the place. Some under different socials and some under different names. I picked up another harassment complaint she filed with the discrimination people. I think your instincts were right on, Dan. I just don't know how you break this news to horny old Boris."

"Keep going, Dan. I'll talk to Sheila and see what she thinks we should do. Stay in touch."

There weren't a lot more places to look, and I didn't know how much more was out there. The criminal records came up with a shoplifting charge for which she paid a small fine. I figured she must have had a real husband somewhere along the line and the divorce records would be interesting reading. They were. I made an ever diminishing list of leads to follow. Then a got an excited call from Tracey who was doing some integrity audits in the financial district. She could hardly contain herself.

"You won't believe this," she squawked. "I was in the Parker House checking the bar. I walked upstairs and almost fell over. Guess who's getting married in the main function room."

"Not you or me, so it's probably of limited importance."

"Wrong. Our friend, Chantal."

"What? Are you sure?" I was stunned.

"There is a poster on an easel in front, with her name and the groom's."

"The groom doesn't happen to be Boris?"

She laughed. "Hardly, it's Clayton Thaxter. Sounds very old Boston. I got a picture of the poster. I tried to go in, but the room is reserved with security and couldn't even sneak in. I did get a look though, before I was stopped and, sure enough, the bride sure fits the description we have. Aside from the poster, I got a list of the events of the day at the hotel, and guess who's listed? The wedding of Chantel Morgan and one Clayton Thaxter, poor sucker."

"Bring it all in. I'll call the client and see if he

knows what's going on."

Sure enough. The posters said Chantel was getting married at the Parker House, which was not exactly second rate digs. I called Don. "We have a photo of the nuptial announcement of Chantel Morgan and one Clayton Thaxter. Know anything about that?"

"Holy shit! You're kidding. I'll be right there."

Don rushed in forty minutes later. He was excited as a kid with his first Playboy magazine. I showed him the photos and a copy of the hotel function announcement. He could barely contain himself.

"I'm going to ask Boris if he knows this. My guess is that he has no idea and he'll fall off this horse."

"Want us to continue the background?"

"For sure. I won't say anything about what you are doing. I'll just bring up this wedding and say someone saw her." He took copies and left like he was going to a chocolate factory.

Two days later, on a chilly cloudy day, Don called again.

"You won't believe this. I told Boris about this and he got pissed. Called in Chantel and asked her. You won't believe what she said."

"Lay it on me."

"She said, with a straight face, that she was a surrogate bride. Said that her girlfriend was the one really getting married, but was afraid of a stalker, so Chantel said she filled in as a surrogate, pretending that she was the bride instead. So, she really didn't get married. Her girlfriend did, but she stood in for her."

I pondered that for a minute. Had not heard

of surrogate brides. I wondered if they had surrogate honeymoons. "That's really good. You have to hand it to her. It takes real balls to tell that story with a straight face. What did Boris say?"

"He bought it. One hundred percent. I couldn't believe it. In fact he complimented her on her courage."

"No fool like an old fool."

"Keep going, Dan. This woman is poison and I've got to expose her."

A week later I was done. I had all of her aliases, her criminal record and the liens and judgments against her. I found she had twice filed complaints for sexual harassment. I had three former employers would not rehire her, in fact one said he would have her arrested if she ever set foot in his place again. The report was as thick as a car catalog.
I called Don and told him it was coming. I asked him to let me know the outcome. He called back the next day.

"Dan, I got fired. Sheila too. We gave the report to Boris. He just glanced at it and started screaming at us. How dare we do this without permission. How dare we slander poor Chantel. He kicked us out."

"What are you going to do?"

"Nothing. I'm glad I'm out of there. That woman is a viper. He's headed for a bad time and I'm better off out of there. And, if everything we did and he has no regard for our intensions or loyalty to him. Well, the hell with him."

I figured I would get some slack from Hovanesian about the report. Didn't care. Dan was good to his work and sent me my fee within a week. Although I had some back door sources, most of what I found was public record and legit.

There is never a happy ending when lies and deceit out weights truth and integrity. However, later on, Boris finally caught her with a hand in his cookie jar and had her arrested. She was found guilty of embezzlement and larceny. You could mess with the old guy's libido, but not his money.

SERIAL LIARS
Some cases are like looking into a row of mirrors.

I was thinking the new girl is nicely racked when the call came in. The female voice on the line was at once sensuous and commanding. She got my attention and my feet came off the desk.

"Please hold for Attorney Pollicari."

It was an instant focus. Tony Pollicari was one of those storied mobster lawyers. Featured in the papers like he owned stock in them, he was always proclaiming his clients' innocence with a subtle wink. I had never met him, but did know some attorneys who knew other attorneys that knew him. He was a big deal.

I put on my best voice. "Dan Hughes, how can I help you?"

After a minute of dead air, a voice, sounding like my uncle on Christmas, came on.

"Dan, Tony Pollicari here. I need your help with a case. It's time sensitive so you have to go right away." He sounded like he was multi-tasking and I was the bottom task. "Call Angie Cicerelli at 617, 555.2110. Tell him you're my guy and help him out. Let me know how you make out. We're going to trial in two weeks so you have to go right away. Thanks."

Click; gone. I just managed to jot down the number. I sat still for a long moment and absorbed it. Pollicari only took high profile cases. I immediately started wondering what I could bill for this. Also, what the hell was this all about and how did he get my number? Such are the mysteries of my daily existence.

A stiff spring wind hissed down Boylston Street, reshuffling papers and debris and forcing women hold down their skirts with token modesty. Boston was busy but never rose to the hustle of New York. Well dressed shoppers mingled easily with the office clericals and businessmen of the neighborhood. I stared out my second floor window at the scrawny tree struggling to come back to life and thought about my work load. That was no problem. I took a look down the hall of our second floor offices. Bob was editing some reports from a couple of undercover investigators. Beth was chatting away on the phone, hopefully to a client, and Robin, the receptionist, was spraying Fantastic on her telephone, getting ready to short circuit it. A couple of phone lines were active, but not exactly ringing off the hook. This definitely was welcome.

Watching a McDonald's wrapper dance in the breeze, I had tried to figure out how a guy like Tony Pollicari had even heard about me. And, who the hell is Angie Cicerelli? I computer researched both names. Pollicari had pages of information. Not a Bruce Cutler but a close second. Seemed to usually defend guys who seriously needed defending. Several names popped out at me; names of guys you don't want mad at you.
Angie Cicerelli was another matter. Took a while but finally found he owned the Taste of Italy pizza shop in Everett. Looked like a big family. Looked like a real Gumba. I called the number.

  A foghorn answered. "Yeah."
  "Mr. Cicerelli?"

"Yeah."

"My name is Dan Hughes. Attorney Pollicari asked me to call. How can I help you?"

"Get right over here. Know where we are? 1422 Bayside Avenue, Everett. How soon can you be here? He sounded like forty years of back room conversations.

"How about an hour?"

"Good, do it." He hung up. No one apparently liked talking on the phone this day.

I map-quested it and got into my sport jacket; glad I wore the good one today. Business cards and pen and paper, the basic tools of today's private eye, went into my pocket and I started out. Everett was close, but most Back Bay Bostonians had not a glimmer of how to get there, nor did they want to. Twenty-five minutes and a different world away, I was on Bayside Avenue, looking for the Taste of Italy pizzeria.

It was a tired street, lined with clapboard triple-decker houses, some with low metal fences protecting litter filled miniscule front yards, others with narrow driveways on the side, just wide enough to squeeze a sedan through. There were several 'Go Sox" signs stuck in first floor windows.

The Taste of Italy was in a weathered grey square building, shaped like on boxcar on end, and seemed to be slightly leaning to one side. Though the name poster filled front window, I could see the ovens in back of a pale white counter, and pictures of Frank Sinatra on the walls. There were a half a dozen Formica tables with a couple of sitters with pages of the <u>Boston Herald</u> opened in front of them. Along the side of the building was parked a midnight black Porsche 911 and beside that was a wooden staircase leading up to what appeared to be an apartment. I went up and knocked.

The door was answered by middle-aged man who looked like a jukebox with feet. "You Hughes? Come In."

I went into was the living room of the residence; cluttered with elaborate couches covered with clear heavy plastic, with ornate lamps on the sides. A plump woman, in a billowing flowering dress, I took to be Mrs. Cicerelli gave me a worried look and left the room. Sitting to one side was a muscular man in his mid-twenties. He had full black hair, good features, highlighted by a heavy gold chain visible behind his opened shirt. He seemed to be highly impressed with himself. This I took to be the younger Cicerrelli.

"Sit down," the older man ordered. I did, and waited.

"This is my son, Sonny," he said, gesturing to the Italian Stallion. I got up and walked over, shook his hand and sat back down on a love seat that crackled under my weight. Sonny looked at me without a word.

"Here's the deal," he began. "My son has been accused by a whore of doing improper things. He's had a little trouble in the past so this could be very serious."

"Serious, like cops or serious like pay-off?" I asked.

"We offered the bitch more money than she deserves and she wouldn't even talk to us. She says she wants Sonny in jail. She's a rotten bitch. I figure she's holding out for more."

I looked over at Sonny, who was eyeing me with half closed lids. "What happened, Sonny?"

"This is privileged, right?" He had obviously been talking to lawyers.

"Discretion is crucial to my business. Whatever you tell me, stays with me. I'm here to help if I can."

"OK. I was in the Squires and she comes on to me like I was the last guy on earth. I couldn't get rid of her."

"Her being?" I shifted on the seat and again it crackled.

"Her name is Kyber Bondi. She's a local ho."

I took out my trusty pad and wrote her name, then Sonny's name and the word "guilty."

He continued without prompting, "We ended up drinking some shooters and she wanted me to take her home. Who am I to refuse?" Sonny was obviously used to spreading his manhood around freely.

"So we go back to her place, and she's all over me. I told her she was too drunk for me, but she wouldn't take no. So, we got it on. She's a pig and she liked it rough. Everything was cool, and then two days later, I'm slapped with a complaint saying I raped her and beat her up. I don't have to rape nobody. She's trying to shake me down." Sonny smiled, confident I understand the problems a guy like him has to face in his life.

"Has she asked for money?" I'm thinking there's more to this story.

"Not yet, but I hear she's shaken down other guys." He settled back as if to say that proves his case.

The old man jumped in. "That's what you need

to do. Find the other guys she's blackmailed so we can use them in the trial."

"Tell me about the trial."

"Sonny's got to go in two weeks. The DA wants him to do time. Its bullshit, but we've got to find some way to show she's a liar and blackmailer. Go find other guys and we can beat this."

I tried to assess what I was getting into. The studly Sonny Cicerelli was lounging back on the couch, very full of himself. The father, big Angie, looked like he was ready to tear the head off a poodle. The room exuded old country Italian, right down to the smell of cigars and the Virgin Mary statue on the buffet. Sonny could be a victim, but it was doubtful. On the other hand, who am I to make these kinds of judgments? I'm supposed to get information for my client. At this point I had no idea how I could possibly find someone else this Bondi babe did, let alone get them to tell me they paid her off to keep her quiet. If that did happen, it stands to reason they would be quiet about it as well. But, being a bit of a ho myself, there was not any doubt I would take this case and see if I could get Sonny's considerable chestnuts out of the fire.

"OK, I'll do what I can. Give me everything you have. Her address, if you have it, her description, where she hangs out, what she drives and anybody else that knows her or anything about this."

Angie growled, "I'll get Sonny to give you all. Just get going and get this bitch what she deserves."

I took down everything they had and took a promise to send me more when they got it. I got up with a final crinkle from the couch, shook hands around and headed back down the rickety stairs into a light rain, and back to the higher civilization of Back Bay.

Revere Beach is accessible by way of the Callahan Tunnel, which makes it somewhat inaccessible. It's got Wonderland Dog Track on one end and Lynn, the "City of Sin" on the other. The beach is known for its icy waters, a famous roast beef stand and the plethora of used condoms and beer can tops mixed in the grey sand. There was a smattering of clubs along the beach and just off. The Squires was off. It's a low, free-standing cinder block building that could be used for automotive repair, dead storage or, in this case, a seedy meet-market club with a long bar along one wall, and a large dance floor overhung with a giant disco ball and surrounded with red vinyl booths, most with tears in the seats. It reeked of longing and despair.

It was after ten when I came in and it was just waking up. Two guys with ball caps and three young women wearing tight tee shirts and jeans were at the bar. A couple of couples were in the booths. It didn't look like a hot night. I sat down and waited for the bartender to stop cutting limes to come over. I ordered a Sam Adams. I gave him my charming smile. "I'm Danny and I'm trying to find a guy a friend owes money to. I heard he hangs around with a girl named Bondi or something. Any idea?"

He looked back with idle indifference. I threw down a twenty for the beer and gently pushed it forward. He brightened a little. "Kyber? She hangs out with a lot of guys."

"I guess this would be someone that doesn't like her anymore."

"That's a lot of guys, too. Last one I knew was Tyke Mandich. He probably hates her more than the usual."

"Could be. Tyke come in here much?" This was promising.

"Here or over at Alibi." He was losing interest. A fifteen dollar tip only goes so far.

"OK, good enough. I'll hang around for a while and see if he shows up. Give me a heads up if he shows."

"Yeah, OK." He was already moving towards the girls who were chattering like parakeets and showing signs of finishing their Cosmopolitans.

I waited through another beer and headed out to The Alibi Lounge. It only took me ten minutes. The Alibi Lounge made Squires look down right upscale. But, it must have had something to offer as the bar was crowded with a lot of twenty some-things. I notice there were more women than men. Must the demographics of Revere. It took a couple of minutes before I could get to a spot at the bar, and another couple for the bartender to spot me. As the beer was served, I asked if Tyke Mandich was around. He was. Two barstools down.

I made my way over and waited for a good time to talk to him. When it came, I leaned over. "Tyke? How you doing? I'm a PI working for a mutual friend. Can we chat for a minute?" I handed him my card.

He looked at me, at the card, and back at me like I was something he did not want to catch. "What's this about?" Tyke was built square, with good shoulders, but with a Jell-O gut. He had a short van dyke that made him look slightly oriental, like someone miscast in a Kabuki theatre.

"I think you have a mutual acquaintance with Manny Cicerelli." It was tough to talk above the DJ and crowd. "Kyber Bondi?" I saw the girl next stool over turn and look at me.

I got his attention. "So what?" He muttered.

"Maybe the same shit, two ways. Give me a chance to give you the full scoop."

I saw his jaw twitch, the scraggy van dyke shaking. I think I had something here.

I gave it a minute, and then said, "Look we can't talk here. Give me a number I can reach you and give it all to you. Nothing about you. Could be worth your while." I was hoping for the best. I signaled the bartender for two beers for us.

He gave me a long hairy look, and then spouted out his number. I was just barely able to jot it down on a cocktail napkin, before he grabbed his new beer by the neck and took a long swallow and shuffled away to the end of the bar and stared up at the ballgame on the television. I finished my beer, and watched the action. I once saw a mating dance between gaggles of wild turkeys on Martha's Vineyard; the action at the bar looked to be about the same.

I called around eleven the next morning. He answered on the fourth ring, so I knew it was his cell.

"Tyke? I'm the guy you met in the bar last night. Possible to catch up for a couple of minutes? Off the record and very, very confidential."

"What's this about?"

"Manny has a problem with the Bondi chick. Thought you could give me some insight to the situation. Strictly confidential and worth your while." I had no idea how it could be worth his while, unless the free coffee I would buy would count.

There was dead air for a minute or two. "Where?"

"Where are you? We can find a nearby coffee shop and chat for a couple of minutes."

"I'm working at Revere Collision off the parkway. Be here all day."

"Isn't there a McDonald's near there? We could meet on your lunch hour."

"Yeah, I get a break at twelve. I got a half hour."

"See you there." With informants, you always hope for the best, but, like a blind date, you're almost always disappointed. Still, it was my only lead so far.

I make it a point to always show up early to scope out the area and watch my person arrive. That way there are fewer surprises and I can select my spot. I bought two coffees and sat in a booth with a view of the incoming traffic. Shortly after twelve, I saw him drive a dark blue Pontiac coupe, with white racing stripes across the hood, into the lot and park. He was alone. That was a good thing.

I got up and met him coming in. "How about some lunch? I was just about to order a Quarter Pounder."

He grunted what I took to be an affirmative reply and we stepped to the counter. We took our combo meals to a rear booth.

I said, "Look, the first thing I want you to know is that this is strictly confidential. It goes nowhere."

Mandich chomped into his burger and eyed me suspiciously. "The Bondi broad is nothing but trouble. If Manny's fucking around with her, it's his problem." He said. A drop of ketchup trickled down his van dyke.

"Manny's being accused of raping her. He tells me she's shaking him down and we're trying to find out if that's possible. I hear you used to go out with her."

"Go out? That's a laugh. I picked her up at the Alibi and we went to my place. She was nutty. Wanted me to pull her hair, do her up the ass and push her around. We went at it for about two hours."

"When was this?

"About three months ago. Anyway," Mandich paused, wondering about me. I nodded, and waited. He sat for a minute, and then went on, "I told her I would call her, but I sort of forgot. Three or four days later, she calls me. Don't know how she got my number. She says I took advantage of her because she was drunk. Calls me all sorts of names and says she's going to the cops." I said, "What the fuck, I did everything you wanted, but she just kept screaming at me. Making all kinds of threats. I didn't want any shit from a psycho, so I sez, what can I do to make it up to you?'

You think it was because you didn't call?"

"Who knows? But she starts yammering about her rent is due, her car payment has to be paid and shit. So I sez, how about I drop off a couple of hundred to make things better and she calms down. Sez she wants five hundred. Sez she'll call my wife. So I end up giving her the five large and stay as far away as I can. She's a total bitch."

"Think that's what happened to Manny?"

"How the fuck should I know? All I know is I did nothin wrong and it ends up costing me five large. Could've got a hooker for half that, with no hassles."

"Let me ask you, Tyke, if it came down to it, would you testify as to what happened?"

He looked at me like he just discovered a boil on his lip. "You funkin nuts? I want nothing to do wid that broad. Manny's an OK guy, but I owe him shit. Forget it. I got to get back to the shop."

With that, he pushed out of the booth and ambled out, leaving me to dump his wrappers and cup. The windows shook when he started the Pontiac.

The good news is that Manny may not be as big a creep as I thought, but the jury was still out on that. What Mr. Mandich didn't know is that he could be subpoenaed into court to testify, which would be helpful, even as a hostile witness. It was an in-field hit with no runs scored. It looked like I'll have to make more bar runs.

The weather turned warm. Spring was rolling in and that fact was reflected in attitudes. For the next six days I got five calls a day from Cicerelli demanding I perform miracles. The trial was looming close and I could tell he was getting very, very afraid. I had no more answers. I bought beers in every joint I could find in range, leaving ten dollars tips to a herd of bartenders. Nothing more developed. Then, while looking sadly at my Visa bill, a call came in.

"Hear you're looking for some information about Kyber Bondi." The voice had twenty years of cigarette static in it.

"Maybe, who's calling?" I was at my usual razor sharp quickness.

"Meet me behind the KFC on Legionnaire Highway in Winthrop today at three. You'll find what I got very interesting" There was a period of dead air, then the dial tone as the caller hung up.

It was a little after one. The lunch crowd was in full swing and the warm sun brought out everyone. "Where are these women in the winter?" I wondered. I sat and thought for a minute. I have one very questionable witness for Manny. Even if he answered a summons, I figured a fourteen year old prosecutor would shred his testimony. So, with nothing to lose, I told Robin I'd be back sometime and went out to my Z that I parked at a meter around the corner. The plan was to get a sandwich, then arrive early to cruise the Kentucky Fried Chicken to scope it out.

Legionnaire Highway was a strip of fast food restaurants, bars featuring Keno signs and pot hole pitted lots with used cars sagging on their springs. The KFC was free standing with a large parking lot behind, pretty much hidden from the street. It was a good place to meet unless the cops had a craving for chicken. I parked down the street at a strip mall that had a view of the restaurant. At ten minutes three, an enormous and aging white Cadillac sedan pulled in and around to the back out of sight. I could see three heads bouncing in the car as it banged into the lot. That had to be my guy. I drove over and cruised slowly into the lot.

The Caddy was as large as a small swimming pool. The back door was open. Standing next to it was a thin, weasely man, with a shaved head and tattoos on his arms that identified him more as an ex-con than if he was wearing stripes. At the rear and front of the car were his two toadies, each about 19 years old, skinny with baggy pants and auras of stupidity. I swung the car around so it was facing out in front of them and got out. The weasel gave me a huge grin as I walked over.

"Danny Hughes," I said, sticking my hand out.

"Benny," he replied. "How ya doin." His hand was damp and weak. I would remember to wash mine thoroughly later.

We shook hands and I pulled him slightly away from his car and sycophants. They stood with practiced indifference, obviously unsure what to do without specific instructions. Benny nodded to them and they remained leaning on the car.

"How can we help each other?" I asked.

"I hear you're trying to help out Manny. I know all about it." There was years of nicotine and cheap booze in his voice.

"Yea, I'd like to help him out, but the clock is ticking."

"She wants to recant her story."

"What? Who?"

"The cunt. The one that's trying to screw Manny."

"You mean Bondi." I glanced over to the two bozos that were trying to light a roach with a match and had forgotten there were other people in the lot. "She wants to drop the charges?"

"Yea, her. She wants to back off but a cop she's fuckin wants Manny bad and won't let her. If she can talk to someone alone, without him knowin, she'll drop the whole thing."

"Really. Tell me about this." I wanted him to run at the mouth so I could gauge if he had any truth in any part of his body. "Let's get a coffee and talk."

"I don't want to go around front so no one sees me. Get them to go and we can talk here."

"Be right back." I figured the price of the coffees was cheap for this conversation.

I brought back two coffees and found Benny sitting in the car talking in melodic tones on his cell phone. If was possible to leer while talking on the phone, Benny had mastered it.

One of the two goons was staring up at the sky and the other was staring at him. They paid no attention to me as I slid into the back seat.

"What have you got?" I was hopeful.

"Here's the deal," Benny started slow, and then got on a roll. "The cunt is fucking an Everett cop who has a hard-on for Manny. She and Manny hook up and she comes home with a split lip and bite marks on her tits. The cop takes a nutty, and starts slapping her around. She tells him not her fault, Manny beat her up."

"Did he?"

"What do I know what happened, but I doubt it. Word around is the rougher the better for her. Hear she travels around with a leash and studded dog collar.

So, the cop talks her into making a complaint against Manny, knowing he will be a three time loser and might go away. Sweet revenge."

"What do you think she will testify against Manny?"

"That's it. She doesn't want to, but she's scared shitless of the cop and he's pushing her. She tells me she wants to back out of the whole thing but needs some kind of protection against the cop. If someone with some juice would cover her, she says she will go away."

"How do you figure in this?" I asked, afraid of the answer. He responded with his leer, and I figured that if he was doing her too, her taste in men was on the dark side of Neanderthal.

"I like her and want to help her out." He was as sincere as a snake oil salesman.

"Can I talk to her? I don't have much time."

"Yeah, let me set it up. I'll call you." With that, he tooted the horn and his two goons jumped two feet into the air from the sound. They hustled over to the driver's window and Benny motioned them in to car. I took this a cue to get out and I stood to the side as the car started up with the subtleness of an enamel and chrome Rhino and chugged out of the lot, its muffler hanging low and banging the curb as it left.

The call came in late the next day. Benny's voice came through like mold on bread. "Meet me at Carmine's in Easty tonight. She'll meet with you."

"What time?" Nothing ventured, nothing gained.

"Ten o'clock.' He hung up. I figured he was in a hurry to get to confession.

Every PI somehow accumulates different characters. Bobby Lamonica was certainly one. A former police officer, Bobby was also the son of a fairly notorious Costa Nostra crime figure. He was fond of saying that one can choose your friends, but not your relatives.

Bobby had a reputation of working two sides of the fence, but I always found him to be a standup guy. He had excellent contacts on both sides, and to say he was street wise was a gross understatement. With film noir hair swept back and chiseled world weary features, Bobby looked like he stepped out of a Godfather movie. Benny didn't give me an exactly warm and fuzzy feeling and it seemed prudent not to go tromping around East Boston in the dead of night by myself, regardless of how inept Benny's entourage seemed. I called Bobby.

He came by the office at nine and we took off in my car, getting into East Boston in fifteen minutes. Carmine's was at the apex of a three-sided corner. It had a long bar up front, tended by a three hundred pound gorilla that hadn't smiled since the Korean War.

The back room, two rows of maroon colored vinyl booths sat, not visible from the bar or the street. Because it didn't close until three o'clock and served a decent pizza until closing, it was a favorite of off duty airline personnel from nearby Logan Airport, and some interesting street people. No one would receive a second glance coming into the place. Bobby and I got there forty minutes early, nodded at the cretin working the bar that seemed to recognize Bobby then sat in a booth in back. The waitress, who ten years earlier may have been a Mediterranean beauty, now sported a roll under her tee shirt and despair under her smile. She came to the table ten minutes after we sat down. Obviously Carmine's was not known for its service. I ordered a scotch, Bobby a black coffee, his sixth of the day.

Benny came in with a flourish a half hour late. He had a ball cap pulled low and was wearing a stained Red Sox sweatshirt. I sat facing the entrance. Benny stopped and squinted, taking a minute to recognize me. He headed over, then paused when he saw Bobby, and then slid into the booth like a wharf rat into a drain. I introduced Bobby and waited. Benny was breathing fast, like he'd been running, a difficult visual to imagine. He took some time to compose himself and get to it.

"She's having sex with a guy around the corner. When they're finished, she said she'll meet with you." Benny waived his hands around to give himself more credence.

"So when do you think that will be?" I asked. Bobby eyed Benny like a mongoose looking at a snake.

"I bet in about an hour. I'll come and get you. Wait here."

"Where are they?"

"Oh, just around the corner. Not far. I'll keep tabs and come and get you. Wait here." With that he slid out of the booth, pulled up his baggy pants and hustled out. Bobby looked at me. I looked back. "I guess we wait a while. What do you think"?

Bobby took a sip of his coffee. "Well, if she meets with you and recants, you'll pull your client's balls out of the fire. Not much to lose. What's your plan?"

"I want to be nice, nice, and get her talking. If she is recanting, I'll try to get a written statement. If she's too hinky to write things down, you and I will have to be witnesses to anything she says that can be helpful."

Bobby sat for a minute. "No problem with me. I got nowhere else to go tonight. Let's get a pizza."

The pizza came and went, the waitress giving Bobby a smile and tit bump as she cleaned the table. I ordered another scotch, Bobby another coffee.

I saw Benny come in again around 11:30. He looked around the bar like he forgot were we were, then came into the back room and oozed into the booth again.

"Well, can we go?" I asked.

"She's really spooked. The guy is hanging around drinking and she doesn't want him to see you. Like I said, she's scared shitless. Let's give it another half hour. Wait here, I'll come and get you." He slid out of the booth and left.

Bobby looked at me. I looked back. "You know, Bobby, I think we should take a look around and see where this asshole is going when he leaves here. He's got a car that you could see from outer space. Shouldn't be hard to find."

"I'm with you partner. Let's go."

We walked out and stood on the street for a minute. Although pushing midnight, there was still a fair amount of foot traffic, mostly stocky men with ball caps going to, or leaving bars. The window lights advertised Budweiser beer and Keno with garish neon. No fat Cadillac in sight.

"Let's drive around a little," I said, and headed

for the car parked down the block.

Driving around, it didn't take long to spot the Caddy, three heads bouncing up and down it as it bottomed across potholes. We dropped back and followed. They circled the block twice, and then stopped at a hole in the wall pizza shop. One of the morons came out five minutes later and passed a flat box into the back seat. I figured this was Benny's epicurean repast as, shortly afterwards; a Budweiser can sailed out of the car, clanking against some garbage cans. We sat in the dark, a block away watching smoke drift out of the car's windows.

Three more beer cans were tossed before the Caddy moved again. It lumbered around the narrow streets like a tugboat adrift. After going in circles for twenty minutes, Bobby said, "This is bullshit, let's go back and see if the asshole shows up."

"I agree," turning away and heading back to Carmine's. Our booth was still unoccupied and we slid back into it to see if Benny returned with any good news. After twenty minutes, he shuffled back in and took a seat next to me and opposite Bobby.

"What's the story, Benny?" I asked straight faced.

"Man, I'm doing all I can. She's really spooked. She says she needs five hundred dollars to move away from the cop and she's desperate, she needs a fix and I got no bread to get it for her. She's hiding out only a couple of blocks from here and says the only person she'll talk to is me. Let me know what you want and I'll work for you."

I looked at Bobby and could see his eyes steel.

The shake down was now obvious. Bobby glanced at me, saw we were thinking the same thing and turned back to Benny. Now, instead of looking around casually, he focused, laser-like to Benny's eyes.

"You wouldn't be fucking with us, would you Benny?" He leaned into Benny, his face a granite mask.

"Shit, no, guys." Suddenly a look of horrified recognition came over him. "Did I see you in the yard? Pause. "Oh, Jesus, you're Ralphie's boy." Benny's complexion faded to a toothpaste white as he realized who Bobby's family is.

Bobby leaned closer into Benny, his voice as dead as a safe door closing. "If you're trying to shake us down, I will reach up your asshole and pull your fucking eyeballs out your ass, and shove them back down your throat." I sat in stunned silence as I saw a stone-cold cobra tear any shred of confidence off of Benny.

Benny's reseeding hairline glistened with sweat and his eyes moved side to side as he digested who he was sitting across from. "Jesus, no. Guys, never. What the fuck. I'd never. I'm just trying to help." He swallowed hard.

We were all silent for a minute. Bobby held his gaze like he was locked onto it. I finally broke it. "OK, let's get a beer and discuss again what we are going to do. I think giving her any money until I hear what I want from her is out of the question."

"Sure, sure. I'll go back and tell her. Maybe I can talk her into seeing you."

"OK, but I want you to wait here for a little while so she starts worrying."

"Sure, sure." Benny looked around. There were no other booths occupied and no where to go. "Let me go to the john. I'll have a Bud. Be right back."

Benny shuffled quickly across the room and disappeared into the men's room.

I looked at Bobby. "That john have a window?"

"I guarantee it."

"Give him five minutes to get away and we'll get out of here. I guess it's not the last time I'll meet a two bit shake down artist." Bobby smiled.

The next day, I told Manny's father that it still looked like the girl was going to testify. That there was possibly a chance she will recant, but I doubted it. I suggested asking for a continuance. He told me they had already three and that the judge had said no more. They were going to trial in two days. No time to find anything else out.

I sat in the last row of Session two of Superior Court, an oval room decorated with an oil of an unidentified founding father hanging over the judge's podium. The trial last four days and Kyber Bondi testified with a shaking voice how Manny Cicerelli held her down, slapped her face over and over, and raped her with force and violence. Although trying hard not to, she still looked like the junkie and part time hooker she was, but that still didn't excuse brutal acts she was subjected to. I found her credible. So did the jury. Manny went away. I lost a client, and felt good about it.

NEVER GIVE UP

Sometimes you get pleasant surprises.

It was a sparkling July morning, heating up to afternoon hot. I had my office window open to the street, catching all the summer noise. I had my feet up on the desk when the call came in. It was Rich, a former prosecutor and was now a spirited attorney in private practice. When he wasn't playing clarinet in back street clubs, he was tossing some cases my way.

"Hey." He was upbeat as usual. "I know you don't much domestic, but I referred you to a client of a client. Don't know much about her, except she supposed to be good people."

"What does she need?"

"Don't know, take it if you want. I asked if she pays her bills and she's supposed to be good as gold."

"Rich, for you, anything"

"You mean for a fee, anything."

"Whatever."

"Her name is Martha Dombrowki. She's got your name."

"OK, why not. What's her number?" He gave it to me. "Where does she live? That number is upstate New York."

"Damn if I know. I just give out the business; hold my breath for any kind of finder's fee."

"If I can find a fee, I might look around for the finder."

"Whatever. Good luck. See you around."

I took the number, thanked Rich and watched two girls in spandex walk down the street before I called. It was answered on the third ring. The woman had the tone of an angry English teacher.

"Mrs. Dombrowski? I waited until she confirmed who she was. She did."I'm Dan Hughes, attorney Richard Miller asked me to call."

"Are you the investigator? I need to talk to an investigator."

"Yes, ma'am, how can I help?" I never away too much information until I knew what I was getting into.

"I need him followed. George. The miserable SOB." She was heating up like the sidewalk outside.

"And George is?"

"George is my husband. He's fooling around on me." The school teacher sounded like she was ready to fail someone for stupidity.

In my business, there were more George's as not. "I'm sorry. How do you know this?"

"He thinks I'm stupid. Thinks I don't have a clue. Well, he's got a lot to learn about me. I check his phone calls, and his little notes to himself. I even know who the little tramp is. Won't he be surprised?" This was one mean woman.

In every domestic case I get, I try to talk the person out of hiring me. If they suspect; they know, whether they consciously admit it or nor. Also, if they only suspect, rather than being confronted with cold, merciless facts, they have options to deal with it. They can ask for a candid discussion with an open mind. They can go into denial. They can wait until the hormones run out and it dies of its own accord. If it's a life altering situation, hiring me won't change anything, anyway. But, I am seldom successful in talking them out of it. They always seem to be hell bent on making themselves miserable by knowing too much.

"Mrs. Dombrowski, if you know what is going on, why you don't just talk to your husband about it. Why do you need me?"

"I want absolute proof so he can't weasel out of it."

I'm thinking George is going to be in deep shit. "If we do get solid proof, what do you want to do, divorce him? You know adultery is no longer exclusive grounds for divorce. Is there a custody issue?"

"Custody? Don't be silly. I just want to make him miserable. I am not going to divorce him so he can be free to fool around all he wants. No, Mr. detective, I'm going to teach George a lesson so he knows he can't get away with it anymore."

I took in a breath of the summer soot and sighed. "OK, Mrs. Dombrowski, we can follow him, find out where's he's going and get video of him. If they're together, we'll get that. But before I commit, where are you?"

"Utica."

"Utica, New York?"

"Yea, Utica. You have a problem with Utica?"

Mrs. Dombrowski, I don't have a problem with Utica, but I'm in Boston. Why don't you get a PI in the Utica area?"

"You think I'm stupid? I asked for a detective in Boston because the fool is going to shack up in

Peabody." She pronounced it Pea-Body, rather than Pee-Buddy, the way we do.

Peabody is better known for its decrepit shoe factories and major highway intersections, than an escape destination for romantic interludes. Paris it's not, but I guess if you live in Utica, Peabody could be a place your dreams and desires are fulfilled.

"So you know he's going to with someone at a motel in Peabody?"

"That's right, and if you don't get moving, we're going to miss him."

"You mean he's going there today?"

"I told you I know what he's up to. He's on his way to the Holiday Inn on Route 1 in Pea-body."

"He's driving to Peabody right now? When did he leave?" Nothing like having to do rapid response.

"He left about an hour ago. He's going to pick up that slut and he's on his way, the bastard."

I did some mental gyrations. Utica was about four and a half to five hours away. If he left about an hour ago, I would have about three hours or so to get one of my guys in position. Peabody's only about forty minutes north of the city. Definitely doable. "OK, Mrs. Dombrowski, I can get someone on surveillance in time. Our fees are $95 an hour, plus $50 for the short notice. This is going to run you about $500. You sure you want to do this."

"I told you, I'm going to make him suffer. I want to do it."

"OK, after you give me the pertinent information, my assistant Rachel will get on the line to take your address and so forth. Now, what does your husband look like?"

"You can recognize him by his walker."

"His walker?" I digested this and paused in thought. "Mrs. Dombrowski, how old is your husband?"

"He's eighty-two." The visual was difficult to bring up in my thought process.

"I see." I said slowly. "And, how old is the woman?"

"She's a young hussy. I think she's around seventy something."

"OK, so I understand. Your husband is eighty-two and he's having an affair with a younger woman, who's around seventy something."

"I wonder if you are really a smart detective. That's what I said." She was getting testy.

"How long have you been married?"

"Fifty five years, and I don't think this is the first time he fooled around. But, now, he's going to pay."

As a private investigator, you supposed to be objective and non-judgmental. Just gather facts. Try not to be too sleazy. But, I think was getting some soft feelings for this guy. But, a client is a client. So, I got the vehicle description, names and her description. Before I set up the surveillance, I used a pretext and found there was indeed a reservation for the subject.

Jason, a part time, streetwise investigator I used from time to time was sitting in the far desk, writing a report. He was a good and savvy surveillance guy. Probably over qualified for this, but I tapped him for it anyway. He thought I was kidding and gave me a goofy look. "You bet, boss," he chuckled.

"Go. You've got about two hours. Get into place and get some video of them checking in. Make sure you get the time and date on the video, do the car and hang around for about two hours after they check in. Let me know."

Off he went, smiling like a contented after glow, carrying his surveillance satchel and a can of Coke, his ball cap on backwards. Five hours went by. I was wondering if Jason really thought I was kidding and went home, when he called.

"Got them." He sounded very happy.

"Where've you been? I should have heard from you three hours ago."

"Are you kidding? They just showed up a half hour ago."

That's about seven hours for a five-hour drive. I had a vision of the car coasting down the New York Thruway at forty miles an hour, the right blinker on the whole way.

"Did you get good video?"

"Are you kidding, it took them fifteen minutes to get from the car to the front desk. I almost fell asleep before he made it. You should have seen the look on the old guy's face. Like he swallowed a canary. I hope he doesn't have a heart attack."

"OK, Jason, hang around for another hour or so. If they leave, tail them. Otherwise, if there is no movement, we can assume they are tucked in for the night. I guess they aren't going to disco tonight."

"Seriously doubt it. The babe had to help him along. She's going to have to help him along for a lot of things. I think he's exhausted already."

I called the client to tell her we had good video of them checking into the hotel. I could hear her glee through the long distance phone call. "Wait till he gets back," she cackled. "I will make his life miserable." I was sure she would. I hope it was worth it for the old guy.

Jason gleefully told the staff and the randy Mr. Dombrowski became a hero in the office. Every guy loved his spirit; the women weren't so sure, but smiled all the same.

LUCKY AND GOOD
The more you move around, the better your chances.

The domestic cases were always the weirdest. On a sultry summer day, an attorney called and put his client on the phone.

"Hi My name is Joel White. I need help."

Mr. White sounded fairly sane, and I knew his attorney so I took out my pencil. "How can I help?"

"Attorney Goodman will verify the long divorce I'm going through. My wife is a bitch."

I had heard these same words many times before. "How so?"

"Not only is she totally ripping me off, she's corrupting our daughter."

Corrupting was a relatively rare accusation. "Really, how is she doing that?"

"My daughter is sixteen, but she looks twenty two, if you know what I mean. My wife is out going to clubs and bars and taking her with her. She's picking up men for them both, buying her drinks and exposing her to all kinds of inappropriate things."

This was a little unusual, but just a little. It sound like something easily verified so I started taking notes.

"Mr. White, we do what we call an activity check. This is basically an intermittent surveillance to determine life style, activities etc. We could do something like this for you, and verify if what you say is happening, and attest to the facts of what we find. If your wife is buying drinks for an underage daughter and exposing her to "inappropriate" situations, we should be able to pick up on that fairly readily."

"That's what I want. Start right away." Mr. White sounded fairly obsessed about this. I should know better. But I took down their names and descriptions, address and vehicle information. The mother drove around in a white Jaguar, courtesy of Mr. White. The description he gave sounded like she fit very well in the car. White had some very clear ideas about what days they were carousing, who they liked to meet and even how they dressed hot these alleged escapades. He never bothered to ask rates.

We were mildly busy and I called in Dino, an excellent surveillance man. Dino was Greek, and looked like a statue you would see in the Acropolis. He eagerly took the assignment. As I had agreed to do intermittent surveillances, over several days, we worked out a schedule for Dino and I basically forgot about it.

I got out a lot and justified it by rationalizing that I got more business from contacts and meetings in bars and clubs, than through any of my direct mailings. It was kind of true, and not a bad rationalization, so I spent quality time in many of the more hip and chic clubs and restaurants in the city. Not a bad way to find business.

During this one particularly beautiful summer night in the city, I was reclining back in a corner booth in one of the "restaurants du jour." With me, were a friend and his very appealing girlfriend. Looking past the dining tables, the scene at the bar looked like a casting call for starlets. They were lined up like a flock of tropical birds, wearing nicely undersized summer dresses. I sipped my martini and leered contentedly. Halfway into my second drink and sinking happily into mellow, I glanced at the entrance and sat up with a start. Here comes Dino, pushing past the doorman, hair mussed and sweating, wearing a Mickey Mouse tee shirt and safari shorts with running shoes. He looked like a little league coach lost at a fashion show. He was flushed and excited. I couldn't tell if he was on the job or had just gone off the deep end.

I jumped up as he scooted past my table. "Dino, what the hell are you doing here being dressed like that?" I exclaimed.

He stopped dead in his tracks and blinked. It took minute for him to compute it was me. "They're here. Look outside. That's their Jaguar with the valet.
"Who's here?" I was starting to wonder if Dino had gotten into the grappa.

"The mother and daughter. I've been following them for the past two hours. Look over there at the bar."

Stepping back behind a young woman standing like a flamingo at Hugh Hefner's mansion, I peeked over her shoulder and searched the bar and saw who Dino was looking at. There, surrounding by the usual preening crowd, was an attractive woman, appearing to be on the sunny side of forty. With her, holding a Cosmopolitan was a knockout blond, appearing to be on the sunny side of twenty. The mother and daughter of the distressed Mr. White. The mother wore a skirt too short for her; the daughter spilling out of the top of her sundress. Both were shod in three inch stilettos, the daughter's with straps that enticingly wrapped upward on her legs. Needless to say, they had drawn attention.

People were starting to look at Dino like they were going to ask him if he was going to take out the trash. It was only a matter of time before some manager type was going to come over and show Dino the exit.

"OK, I'll take it from here," I told him. "You break off and put down your time. I'll finish up the surveillance."

Dino looked at me with grateful eyes. He gave a sweaty smile and made his way out the door. With him went my relaxing and happy buzz. My friend in the booth shrugged.

I told him I'd try to get back later and made my way to the bar. Shouldering through the crowd, I wound up standing behind and almost between my two subjects. I forced myself to stop peeking down the enticing front of the daughter's dress and got into my faux Brad Pitt charm mode. Flashing my best smile, I politely asked the mom if I could order a drink from the bartender through them. She gave me a smile back. A good first step.

It took a while to get a bartender's attention and I used the time to size up my quarry, while they pretended to ignore me. The mother and daughter were in full predatory mode, each sizing up the talent while chatting together. Mom was sipping wine, the daughter almost finishing her Cosmo. It should be illegal for a sixteen year old to look like that. Any testosterone infused male would never bother to ask for proof of age from this young lady, but would simply thank the Gods for his good fortune. When I finally got my drink, I apologized to them for reaching over and considered my opening line. Never good at that, I finally blurted out, "Gorgeous night, isn't it?" then winced at my corniness.

The mother turned more toward me and gave me a half wince back. OK, I figured this was good enough and I plowed forward.

"Are you guy's sisters? You look alike."

"Thanks, but this is really my daughter," she replied.

"Come, on. That's impossible unless you got married at twelve."

"No, really," she said, giggling a little.

"My name is Steve," I said, sticking my hand out.

"I'm Sarah, and this is Rachel," indicating her daughter.

I shook hands with both, trying to keep my eyes above her neck... I knew how old she was and was a little bothered by my lust that was mixed with guilt. I was sure that, if she bent over, she would probably spill out. I smiled into her eyes.
"Can I buy you guys a drink?"

They looked at each other with knowing eyes. There was obviously some unspoken communication between them.

"Well, I'll have another Chardonnay. What about you, Rachel?"

"I'll have a Cosmopolitan." I detected the beginnings of the slurred speech of a young girl on her way to intoxication. I wondered if this was entrapment, or if I was an accessory. I decided that I was getting too close to the point of our surveillance and decided to go back to strictly observing and reporting. So, I turned to the guy next to me. He looked like Forest Gump in an Armani suit. Probably good money; probably a loser.

"These are my friends, Sarah and Rachel. They deny it, but expect they are sisters." I gave him a coy wink and he bought into it. He stuck his hand out to them.

"Hi, I'm Hugh," he said.

I said, "Hugh, I think these lovely women are here to enjoy themselves and good male company would help that out. Buy them a drink to keep the party going."

Hugh was only too happy to accept my gift. He immediately signaled to the bartender to bring another round for the women and I stepped discreetly back a foot or so. Sarah had an eye for money and saw right away that while Hugh looked like an ad in GQ, while I was closer to Field and Stream. Her attention shifted away from me and she lit Hugh up with a hungry smile. Rachel was finishing her Cosmopolitan and had another one backed up on the bar. I figured she was on her way to at least a nice throw up, if not a pass out. I realized Mr. White was right. Mom was using her daughter as bait, for whatever purpose.

I pulled out a small camera I had with me. "Smile guys." I said and took a picture before they had a chance to object. "I'm going to send this to my brother in Cleveland to show him how hot Boston is," I lied. The two women gave me a wary smile; Hugh, a stupid grin.

I continued to hang around on the outskirts of this action, mentally documenting the number of drinks Rachel was putting away and watching mom push her forward towards Hugh, and then Hugh's friend who returned from the men's room to what he figured was the jackpot. I then slipped back to my table, where my friends were preparing to leave. I bid them goodbye and set up with a nice line of sight to the White family and the panting hyenas surrounding them. They all finally left together, three rounds later. Hugh was holding up Rachel while peeking down her dress. She had obviously lost her sea legs and Hugh was guiding her through the crowd like he was holding the Holy Grail. Mom was arm in arm with the friend. They all piled into the Jaguar and sped off. While I couldn't tail the Jag to see the conclusion of this happy meeting, I did have a very juicy report, and a very interesting photo, for which Mr. White was grateful and duly presented to the court.

BEING A PI CAN BE PRETTY SLEAZY

Sometimes you just want to take a shower.

Ninety percent of my work was corporate investigations. Those cases can be interesting, but are usually as boring as a TV network crime show. Motives are greed, revenge or stupidity and the culprits sometimes wind up whining in criminal court or in the unemployment line. I have a good moral high ground when working these cases; some domestics, not so.

Over the years, we've worked for some companies steadily and had become friendly with the CEO's and owners. One morning I got summoned to the office of one such executive, a gentleman of high integrity and class whose company I'd helped many times over the years. I would bend over backwards to help any way I could.

The office floor was covered in ankle deep, snow-white carpeting, and the walls were decorated with recognized politicians and athletes. Ira's desk was polished chrome and mahogany and was clean except for two telephones and a blotter. I sat down in a wine colored leather guest chair and said my usual, "How can I help?"

"Dan, I hate to ask this, but it's my brother." He said. "I know you don't usually do these but I need someone discreet and I can completely trust."

"Ira, we've been doing business for a lot of years, now. I'll help with whatever you need."

He was silent for a minute while I sat. Then he turned and looked out at his parking lot with the two hundred cars and took a deep breath.

"My brother Steve lives upstate New York. He's done very well and is in a business much like mine. Well, a couple of years ago, he married a Philippine woman. He's convinced she's taking complete advantage of him, including screwing around. They live in a small town and, of course, everyone knows of her and sees her around. She's embarrassing him and our family name."

Here was coming another possible divorce case, but I was committed. "Want me to find out what she's up to?"

"Exactly, I need you to go there and do," he paused, "I guess what you call an activity check. I'll take care of your fees and expenses. Whatever you find, just pass it on to me and I'll give it to my brother. Bill me for your fees and expenses."

"How much does he need to know?" I asked.

"Spend as long as you need. Just do your good work."

Two days later, a duffle bag with gear in the back seat, and a thermos of coffee in front, I headed out. On the Mass Pike to New York Thruway, I then exited onto a narrow two lane. The hills upstate New York are made for brooding, worn round by long snowy winters and scorching August harvests. It made me melancholy. I drove for forty minutes, past red barns surrounded by indifferent dairy cows and rusted farm equipment and came into the picturesque town of Mohant. On the outskirts, I drove past the usual McDonald's and Burger King, competing opposite each other for five o'clock family dinners. The single road wound into the village center, four blocks adjacent a postage stamp sized green, sporting a freshly painted band stand and an ancient black cannon pointing up into the summer sky.

Traffic was light, and I noticed the majority of cars were Volvos and heavy Lincolns. No industry could be seen, but the town was obviously affluent. I drove around for an hour, orientating myself to the geography, then headed out to Syracuse, an hour away, and found checked into a Marriott. Eating alone in the faux nautical dining room, I made my plans for my surveillance, making sure my video and still cameras were in good shape, batteries charged ready to go, I had binoculars, two small tape recorders, three different ball caps and two jackets, one blue, one red. I also had a pair of glasses with clear lenses and a lunch pail.

I rented a Pontiac sedan for the New York plates, making sure it was as innocuous as I could get and still have some power. The next morning, after coffee and scrambled eggs from the buffet, I headed out. The sun was tangerine, rising up over mists that still clung to the hill tops. There was hardly any traffic.

My client's house was a rambling contemporary perched over an alpine lake. It was off a narrow country road with neighbors a hundred yards away on each side. Cruising by, I saw the drive to the garage slope steeply down fifty feet from the road. The garage door was closed and the house looked silent. I could see a wide deck cantilevered out towards the lake on the opposite side. I figured there were only a handful of houses on the road, all of which seemed to be encroaching wealth into the farm lands. I didn't anticipate much traffic. After four drive-bys, I set up a static surveillance spot in a turnaround a quarter of a mile up the hill. I couldn't see the house, but I could see any cars leaving the driveway. I slouched down and tried to look invisible.

The sun rose higher, as did the temperature. Insects buzzed around the adjacent field and a woodchuck stuck his head up fifty feet away and looked at me with hostility. At eleven o'clock, a silver grey Mercedes sedan pulled out and drove rapidly down the hill. I took off and got it in sight five minutes later. I had both sun visors down and was wearing a Yankees ball cap. I could see someone short with black hair was driving. I was on my surveillance.

I stayed with her for the next five hours. The first stop was a shop called *Hair Affair,* where I got my first good look. She was about five feet tall with a little extra weight in her bottom and legs. She was wearing a white tee, snug tight and a short black skirt and sandals with clunky heels. The light caught the gold on her wrists and neck. She seemed full of herself.

An hour later, she was out and made stops to grocery, hardware and a gas station. The whole day took about five hours and by four o'clock, she was back home and I was again slouched down and cramped in the car. I sat there for another two hours, then, after a couple of suspicious looks from passing cars, started making drive bys. By nine o'clock, I was running out of gas, patience and the feelings in my legs. I headed back to the Marriott.

I was back again the next morning, just a little

later than the day before. My target did not seem like an early riser. Surprisingly, the Mercedes pulled out a little after nine. Again the hound was after the rabbit. This time she drove quickly to a large fitness and tennis club, just outside the center of town, sitting regally in the center of its own lot, with a scattering of cars, mostly foreign, parked in front. She parked next to a green Miata and popped out her car wearing a white tennis top and skirt, the later short and swinging around her hips. She carried a black bag shaped like a pork chop. As a trained detective, I surmised she was going to play tennis. I parked in a far corner, slouched and waited.

Two hours, and one sneaky pee later, she came out, a towel across the back of her neck. I was a good distance away, but could still see the flush and glisten of exercise. The Mercedes sped back into town, but instead of taking the country road up the hill to her house, she swung left, out of town and, surprise, pulled behind the McDonald's. I parked in front, and went in as a customer, getting into a booth were I could see her. She sat in the car, the windows up. Then, five minutes later, the green Miata pulls in and parked next to the Mercedes. The driver, a tall, tanned, good looking guy, in tennis whites, got out quickly and into the Mercedes. I barely had enough time to slide out of the booth, scoot out the front door and get into my car to follow. I ended up the car behind them at the next red light. I saw the top of her head and the tennis guy leaning over her like he was peering down her top. Then his head disappeared into her lap. Again, as a trained detective, I sensed a clue. They make a quick stop at Chester's Wine and Liquors, and then drive up the hill from town to the house. I tail and drive by looking out of the corner of my eye as the garage door closes behind them.

    I got back to my spot and tried to look invisible again. Hours passed with nothing to see or do. The sun turned orange and fiery and dropped down over the lake, creating colorful shimmering on its surface, as the dusk settled in. A car I'd seen before cruised by slowly, the driver giving me a hairy eyeball. Anxiety set in with my leg cramps and hunger pains, but I hung in. Being a PI is dealing with long periods of boredom, interrupted by shorts bursts of heart pounding terror. I was into the boredom phase. By ten o'clock, there was still no activity and I had to leave. I grabbed fast food on the way back to the Marriott, took a long shower and got about three hours sleep. I was back doing slow drive-bys at the already warming dawn. The patience and boredom paid off. At around eight thirty, as I was coasting down the hill, the Mercedes pulled out. Two people were in it. A short woman driving and the guy from yesterday slouched in the passenger seat. It was a short ride from the house to the McDonald's, where she drove past two hundred yards, pulling into the parking lot of the IGA store. He got out and ambled back to the restaurant. She drove away fast. I didn't bother to follow her and I was delighted to see he was wearing the same clothes as he was yesterday. Instead, I tailed him to the tennis club, and I followed him inside a couple of minutes later.

    A fresh-faced Gidget type smiled at me when I asked about membership. She was pleasantly helpful, especially when she described the resident tennis pro and showed me a brochure with his picture on the front. I thanked her, gave a final glance to her perky chest and pocketed the brochure.

I was dog-tired and found Chipper's Diner ten minutes later and treated myself to a truck driver's breakfast. After the second cup of coffee, I called Ira.

"Good morning, it's me, Dan," I said, rather stupidly.

"Hi Dan. What have you got?" He sounded depressed.

"She's shacking up with the local tennis pro. Kind of a classic situation. And, the ugly part is that she is shacking up in Steve's house. He spent the night there last night. His name is Frank Renalds and he looks to be about thirty five or so. They are making a feeble attempt to be discreet, but, if I figured it out in two days, the entire town must know."

"God damn it." I heard him swear into the phone. "I'll get a hold of Steve and let him know. Call me back later."

I went low key and killed a couple of hours out of sight. In the called back,
Ira sounded even more depressed. "Steve is really upset. He wants complete proof because he wants out. Can you get a video of them in the house?"

I thought about window peeping. "No way that I can see in."

"How about from inside the house?"

"How could I do that?" I had an image of me breaking in and hiding in the closet like in a sleazy

Italian movie.

"The housekeeper comes every Thursday. Steve trusts her. She could let you in and maybe you could hide a camera."

I was dreading this more and more. "Possible. I would have to come back and get the equipment. Tell Steve to let the housekeeper know that I will probably come by next Thursday, if our friend is busy elsewhere. I'll line up the equipment and go back next week."

"OK. Do it. Let me know."

I drove back to Boston, got together a time lapse VCR, and a pin hole camera and hand held monitor and cables. I had no idea where I was going to secrete this gear, or even if it would work. The house was a Frank Lloyd Wright type contemporary and I suspected it had few if any real nooks and crannies. And, because the equipment had to sit there for an extended period of time, I needed a power source. I figured an extension cord draped across the living room had a good chance of being noticed.

I called the house the following Thursday Morning. It was set up that when the housekeeper answered, I would ask for Mr. Thaxter. If the wife was gone for a while, she would respond, "There's no Mr. Thaxter here." If she was home, she'd say, "I expect him later." The house keeper clued me that the coast was clear. I drove to the driveway and, as I pulled up to the garage, its door opened and I slid the Pontiac inside and out of sight. The housekeeper, with a low center of gravity in a Mumu, was standing at the inside door, eyeing me like I was a lizard she found in her kitchen.

"Hi, I'm Danny." I said in my cheeriest game show host voice.

"Ugh." She replied as I unloaded my gear.

"Can you show me around?" I smiled.

"This way." She led me into a broad living room with a glass wall looking out to the deck and lake. It was furnished with low white leather Italian furniture and colorful framed paintings, I suspected were originals of somebody. I followed her through the living room and into the master bedroom, about twenty feet by twenty feet, with a cathedral ceiling. I looked up and saw a vent.

"Can I see what's up there?" I asked Helga, the mistress of discipline.

She led me to a rear staircase that led up to a small storage room, in what would be normally an attic. I saw a small door, about four feet by four feet, in the wall to a storage area, opened it and looked in. On the far wall I could make out thin slivers of light. Crawling in, I pushed aside some stored suitcases and squeezed my way to the vent. It looked out into the bedroom, a forty-five degree angle down to the bed. It couldn't be better if I had on black socks, a sleazy moustache and a velvet smoking jacket. That's me, Dan the porn king.

I set up the equipment, inhaling dust and mites. An hour later, the camera was hot glued in place, and I tapped into a small light fixture for the power. I connected my mini-monitor and turned on the VCR. A clear shot of the love platform. I set the timer for seventy-two hours, crawled out, dusted myself off and headed out. I came back three days later and changed the tape. After that,

I had a guy from the office make the trip and swap the tapes until I had six of them. I never looked at them, except to make sure there was something on them.

I gave them all to Ira, saying I didn't know what was on them, but there was nothing more to do. He grimaced at the tapes and me. He put them in his desk and said, "Send me a bill."

A couple of weeks later I happened to ask him if Steve was satisfied with my surveillance.

"Dan, he stacked the videos up on the table and called in his wife. He told her he had his attorney draw up a very generous divorce agreement. He put that on a table next to the stack of videos. He said to her, "You can sign, or we can look at these videos together." He said she hesitated for a minute, and then signed the agreement without a word." He grew quiet and looked at me sadly. "It's over for them. She packed up and left the next day. The funny thing is Steve never looked at videos. I never did and you never did. Who knows what was on them?"

"What did he do with them?" I asked.

"Gone, destroyed. Could have been blank for all she or anyone knows. Good job."

Later, musing about all that I went through and the grungy feeling I had about myself, I realized none of it was necessary. All Steve would have had to do is stack a half dozen or so of video tapes on the table, pretend they were secret evidence and he would have had the same result. Obviously, neither party had any equity in the marriage, and the break up could have been done with more dignity.

It did not stop me from sending my bill. It was paid in five days.

HE DID TWO THINGS GOOD. THE SECOND WAS PLAYING GUITAR

This case was before the advent of DNA testing and is memorable as an example of the folly of human nature.

Her voice was a soft as ten yards of Egyptian cotton, so I had high hopes as I settled into the booth in the faux colonial coffee shop that was stuck out of place in a dusty strip mall outside of Revere beach. As usual, I made sure I was twenty minutes early so I was orientated and comfortable. It was in the middle of the afternoon and what lunch crowd there was all gone. Only me and a retired guy reading the sports page of the *Herald* remained, so she was obvious when she stepped in and stopped to look for me. Instead of a femme fatale, she had unfortunate hips and wore a JC Penny dress with comfortable shoes. She reminded me of my Aunt Edith. She looked at the retired guy, and then at me, and pondered until I waved her over.

She slid nervously into the booth and said, "I'm the one that called. I'm Mary Ann Potello."

"Yes," I replied. I waited.

"I work for the post office."

"Yes," I said, and waited some more. She worked at a small smile and sat quiet. "How about a coffee or tea?" I asked.

"Coffee would be good." Her voice was so soft it was hard to hear. I waved over the waitress who was oddly dressed as a pilgrim, but with white running shoes under her gingham dress. She came right over, grateful for something to do, and served a fresh coffee to Mary Ann and refilled my cup.

"How can I help?" I tried to look hopeful.

She took a sip of her coffee and a deep breath. She seemed to settle down a little.

"You are supposed to be very good," she said. She was one of those plain looking woman who, with a make over, could be fairly attractive. I guessed her in her late thirties, a working woman, plodding through life as best she could.

"It's kind of a long story."

"That's OK. That's what I'm here for. Tell me how I can help."

"Well," she started. "I was married to a police officer. I was pretty young when we got married, and, I guess, not very experienced. She paused and took another sip. I was quiet. "I thought things were going along fine. We were married for four years. Frank didn't want any kids, but we had a little girl, Samantha. She's wonderful. We bought a little house with a yard. Then, one day, out of the blue, he says he was leaving. He packed up that day and left. Turned out he had another girl friend, and even had a baby with her. I had no idea. So, after a while we got divorced and he never came back."

"Was it a difficult divorce? Was there a fair property split?"

"I guess so. I was numb the whole time. I just couldn't believe it and went along with whatever they said. All I know is all of a sudden I was alone in the little house with Samantha. That was three years ago."

"Are things OK now?"

"Well, it was sort of ok, but it went downhill

again."

"How can I help?" I waited some more.

"I guess I have to tell the whole story." She took a deep breath to fill her lung, and then let it go with a long sigh. She stared out the window for a minute. "After Frank left, I just went along working and not doing much. A couple of years went by. Then, one of my girlfriends from work talked me into going out to a club with her. I guess I was pretty lonely by then. Anyway, we went to this club and there was this guitar player and singer there. His name was Doc. He sounded so beautiful. He was magical. After he sang, he came over to our table and talked a while. I guess I had a lot to drink, because the next thing I know, Doc is home with me." She paused and glanced up with a half smile. "Doc could do two things really good; one was playing his guitar."

"So, you took Doc home and had, I gather, a pretty good time."

"Better than pretty good. By the next week, Doc moved in with me. It turned out that he really didn't have any place to live. In fact, I learned later on that he never even paid any taxes, and he never really worked, except to play his guitar."

"OK, now you and Doc are cohabitating." I figured this is where I hear Doc may be cheating on her.

"Well, it really didn't work out how I hoped. Doc didn't like even think about work. So, he never did. I would get up at five in the morning to go to work. I work at the post office. Doc would have just gotten back from whatever club he was playing in. He'd sleep most of the day, then get up and make a baloney and white bread sandwich. Doc liked baloney on white bread with mayonnaise."

Doc didn't seem to be a knight in shining armor and certainly not a connoisseur. She was silent for a moment and sipped her coffee. She said, "I'd get home and the place would be a mess. Doc never picked up anything. Dirty clothes would be everywhere, dishes were piled up in the kitchen and Doc would be sitting there picking at his guitar, with the TV on. Even so, I guess I felt like it was better than before when I was alone."

"None of my business, but it doesn't seem like made in heaven." She ignored the comment.

"Then, out of the blue, Doc says that he ran into an old girlfriend. This old girlfriend tells Doc she had his baby which is now six years old and that Doc should do the right thing and move in with her because he's the father."

"So did he? Jump from you to her?"

"Yes. But she's a lying bitch. I don't think the baby is Doc's. I think she just is saying that to get Doc into her bed."

I'm thinking this Doc must have some technique.

"I asked Doc if he was sure the baby was his and he says he doesn't remember. Doc tends to take drugs sometimes. So I said, to him how could be just dump me after living with me for almost two years and go to this other woman. He says he has to do the right thing for the little boy."

"So, what do you want me to do?"

"I want you to prove the baby is not Doc's so he comes back to me."

"I think only God has the definitive answer to that."

"I think this slut is just looking for someone to support her and Doc's is just too nice a guy."

I am thinking that things must be pretty bad to lie to get a guy who doesn't work, doesn't pay taxes and is hard pressed to know where he is, to support you. What are they both thinking of?

"I've saved up some money. I'll pay you five thousand dollars now and however more I will owe you when you finish."

"Mary Ann, you seem like a really nice woman. Are you sure you don't want to just walk away from this and go on with your life?"

"No, I have to know that Doc is being manipulated by that bitch. I have to show him he's wrong just to leave me like that."

She was on the verge of tears. Her shoulders were sagging like empty sacks and I could see a quiver in her lip. I am never ceased to be astounded by what people get themselves into.

"Tell you what, Mary Ann. Tuck your money away. I'll sniff around and see if there is any possible way of helping. Do you have a picture of Doc?"

"I could only find one." She was fishing deep into her vinyl bag and came up with a wrinkled envelope. "Doc would dress up for the block parties for the kids. This is the only picture I could find of him" She handed over the envelope and I pulled out the photo. Doc looked to be about 5'4" and was in full Bozo the Clown regalia, from the big red nose to the rouged cheeks to the goofy hat. He had stick on elephant ears and size forty shoes. This was not going to be easy.

Mary Ann got into more details. Right after Doc was lured away; Mary Ann still needed a baby sitter from time to time so she enlisted the help of Doc and his new/old girlfriend, Rhonda. It continued to get complicated. She even hinted of a ménage à trois, but I chose not to go down that street.

I got the rest of the information from her and said I would call in a couple of days. Apparently, according to Mary Ann, Rhonda was the town pump in Salem. Doc was just one of a string of happy guys. He was tagged by her to be the fall guy and was dumb enough to accept it.

I sat the next day in my office, contemplating this case. As both Rhonda and Doc were from Salem, I could just see myself walking around with the picture saying, "Do you know this clown?" It was hard to concentrate on my second floor window view as I wondered why I had gotten into this. Clearly, Mary Ann was a nice lady, if more than a little confused about the mysteries of life. This seemed like a domestic puzzle more vexing than the usual and I struggled on how to start. If Doc was the depositor of the seed spawning Rhonda's entry into motherhood, I had to go back at lest six years. If Mary Ann's description of Doc was accurate, he would have a hard time remembering yesterday. So, I stuck the picture of Doc, the clown, on my desk lamp and started drawing a time line. It seemed the key to this was Rhonda's alleged reputation of rounded heels and the fact that this murky stew originated in a small town.

So, I headed up to the leafy town of Salem, on the lookout for any lingering witches, and found the town library set back in front of a lush lawn. It was whitewashed and regal and looked hardly used. Inside was a librarian who appeared to have kept the witches' genes hostage and eyed me suspiciously as I shuffled in. I probably should not have worn the blue blazer over the black tee shirt. A little too Miami Vice for a small town. But, after beaming out my most charming detective smile, I was pointed to the school yearbooks by a crooked finger.

Searching through ten years of smiling faces, I came up with Rhonda. "Rhonda Polanski, no activities, hoping to open her own hair styling salon; *Girls just want to have fun.*"

No Doc, although there was a photo of a sophomore band with a short grinning troll in the background. I suspected Doc was not academically inclined and so never finished high school. I sat down in a corner and made a list of all names for the year before and the year after Rhonda's graduation, snuck behind the librarian at the gate and swiped a town and surrounding area phone book. Stashing them under my snappy blazer, I breezed by the front desk returning the icy glare with smile and headed back to the dirty air and traffic of the city.

For all of its village appearance, Salem High had pretty good-sized classes and I ended up with over a hundred names. Some I culled out, figuring anyone involved in the math club, or religious studies would not have run in Rhonda's circles. I contemplated the jocks and put them on the call list, as the raging testosterone of these guys would have definitely sniffed out Rhonda if her reputation was true. I ended up with eighty-three names and started searching through the phone books for them. I had to figure most of the girls now had married names so I ended up with four different lists of ascending interest.

Telephone canvassing is as interesting as eighty miles of cornfields. Plus, you have to be upbeat and charming on the phone not to get angry hang ups before you can get out your spiel. I found having a cup of coffee handy for sipping and a closed door helps. The first twenty eight calls were either no answer or voice mails. Where I could, I left mysterious messages hoping they would be intrigued enough to call back. I did get three women in the next fifteen calls that had recollection of Rhonda, but no knowledge of her escapades.

One of the classmates was Marion O'Connor. I found a M. O'Connor in the Lynn directory and tried it.

"Hi, I'm trying to help a person with some personal problems and I was wondering if you remember Rhonda Polanski?"

"I remember her. Who is this?"

"Honestly? I'm a private investigator working on a domestic situation and I was trying to find a guy Rhonda was seeing about six or seven years ago." I tried my best silver voice.

She laughed for a good minute. She had a robust laugh and I knew I would like her and knew she would probably be straight with me, if I could get her to talk. I laughed a little with her. "What I found so far is I may have several candidates."

"More like a gaggle of them. Rhonda liked to party."

"Did you know her well?"

"Sort of. We knew a lot of the same kids." There was a pause and I thought I was losing her. "I don't like talking on the phone to someone I don't know."

"Don't blame you. Maybe there's a coffee shop nearby we could meet for a cup of coffee. At your convenience. It would be very appreciated if you could help, even a little bit."

"I don't know." But I could tell she was intrigued. "You say you're a private eye? Like on television?"

"Well not exactly. I avoid car chases and gun battles and hardly ever meet beautiful blondes that are interested in me."

She laughed beautifully again. She was coming back.

"OK, there's a McDonald's on Lynn Shore Drive. I'm going to do some errands and will be near there around three o'clock."

"You're terrific. See you there at three. I sort of look like what I am. Easy to spot."

"OK. I'll have fifteen minutes."

Lynn Shore Drive is a jumble of used car lots, discount stores and fast food, winding north from Revere and ending at the edge of the rusting and down and out City of Lynn (Lynn, Lynn, city of sin). If you swing right, the drive brings you to the entrance to Nahant or north along the sea towards Swampscott. The short run along the sea is this side of spectacular, with large homes from another, more prosperous era, on the left, overlooking the gun metal beach and Egg Island, named for obvious reasons, sitting a quarter mile out. The City of Lynn is like the drug addict that, no matter how hard it tries, is a loser. I found the McDonald's twenty minutes early and settled in with a copy of the *Herald*. Fifteen minutes later, I saw her come in. She was tall and very well put together, wearing the Lynn fashion of tight jeans and a Red Sox tee shirt. Her hoop earrings dangled to just above her shoulders. I appreciated that she was not wearing a bra. I waved her over, and she clacked over in her high heel sandals.

"Hi, I'm Dan," I said, stranding with great chivalry.

She looked me up and down and, with tacit approval slid into the booth. "Can I get you lunch or coffee?" I asked.

"A coke I guess." She looked like someone you would pray to meet just before closing in some club. I took the opportunity, while standing at the counter, to check her out. I decided that, if she knew something, she would be helpful.

I brought over the coke and a coffee for me and gave her a winning smile. She smiled back.

"You're kind of what I expected," she said.

"Yeah, it's kind of like a man and his dog. After a while they look alike. More and more I look like what I do."

"So, what's this about Rhonda?"

"Have you seen her lately?"

"No, I know she's around because people see her. I don't run in her crowd and I don't want to."

"Her crowd is not so good?"

"Dopers and creeps, what I hear. Of course, it's probably not surprising." She smiled and it was a version of the laugh I heard on the phone. Very appealing.

"Please keep this confidential, "I said. "Rhoda says that Doc, the guitar player is the father of her child, and I'm trying to figure out if that's true."

She laughed out loud. "Doc? That little Charley Mason type? I doubt he has anything big enough to knock anyone up." She laughed again.

"Well, that's why I'm around. It does seem rather implausible. But, if not Doc, who?"

"Could be anyone of a dozen." She looked into her coke and thought for a minute. "You know, who might know is this little dude that hangs around the liquor store that's on Salem Common. I think his name is Dudley, or maybe Dork." She laughed again at her joke. Women with a sense of humor are the sexiest.

"He hangs around the liquor store?" I asked.

"I think so. I think they give him free booze to sweep up and carry in the cases. He is one human basket case. He might even live on the Common. I think even he was doing Rhonda."

That was all she could give me and I thanked her. She pushed her half finished coke aside, gave me another smile as wide as the Charles River, and stood up. "You have my number if you need any more information. I'm usually around every morning after ten."

After a brief eye-to-eye contact, she turned and strode out. I admired the swing of her backside as she left. It took me another five minutes of sipping my coffee and musing before I could leave. I put her number in my book.

I waited until the middle of the afternoon the next day to head back to Salem. I figured anyone who basically lived at a liquor store was not an early riser. I found Park Spirits on the north side of the common, sandwiched in between a coffee shop and a hairdresser. It looked like Dudley had all he needed, booze, coffee to sober up and a salon to shape up. I tried the coffee shop first. It was something that was designed years ago, before the advent of fast food restaurants. It had a long counter, with a dozen or so red vinyl topped stools lined up perpendicular to the front door, with a couple of Formica tables opposite. Most of the stools had tears in them. Behind the counter was a hefty woman in a pale blue smock with extra wide lipstick. I sat down and picked up the menu that was stuck on end next to the pie display. The server ambled over and served coffee without asking. I ordered a grilled cheese sandwich. The order was taken with supreme indifference. When it was served, I brought up my winning smile again and caught her eye.

"Know where Dudley is today?" I asked.

"Probably where he is everyday when he's not mooching food from here, either hauling cases or sleeping."

"Think he's next door?"

"Either there or on the bench he calls home."

"Where's the home sweet home bench."

"Towards Main Street, on the left side of the common. He could be sitting there or just getting up."

"Thanks." I said. I felt obligated to finish my sandwich which was warm Velveeta on white bread. I figured it would remain deeply imbedded in my stomach for the rest of the day. Washing it down with the rest of the three hour old coffee, I winked at the server and left a two dollar tip. No sense in coming on too strong like Mr. Big Shot from the city.

The common was as pleasant as a summer poem, with ancient trees shading the benches. Aside from a couple of women pushing strollers and two guys throwing a Frisbee, it was quiet. I walked in the direction given and, shockingly, saw a skinny guy with a scraggy goatee sitting with a newspaper on his head. I figured he was either looking for shade or had given up reading and was hoping he could absorb the news directly through his cranium. I sat down next to him. He was barely aware of my presence.

I figured that there was no reason to try to con this guy as he was beyond conning. So I turned abruptly and said,"Dudley, I'm a private eye. I need some information from you and I will give you fifty dollars to talk to me. How about it?"

He looked back at me with gimlet eyes. I could tell he was having trouble processing. Finally, "What?"

"Dudley, you are sort of the mayor of Salem." I figured compliments would go a long way. "You can help me with information. And, I can help you with money."

That seemed to get through. It took a while. His face brightened and he almost smiled.

"What do you want?"

Remember Rhonda? From school? She says that Doc is the father of her kid, and now Doc is on the hook for support."

"Doc? Rhonda? Oh, yeah, that's funny. When are we talking about?"

"A good six or seven years ago." I was worried that his brain didn't go back that far.

"Nah, Rhonda's been screwing Karl Hackney for a long time now. Put her out of circulation. Last time I tried to hook up she said Karl would kick my ass. But, I hear he's in the slammer. That's probably why she grabbing what she can."

"You think the timing's right, that Karl might be the father of her kid?"

"Yeah, Karl's been porking Rhonda for years. He's been living with her off and on. Someone told me he knocked her up a while back. But I'm pretty sure he's in the slammer."

"Why's he in?"

"They caught him breaking into a house. He's a biker and probably needed parts. Was about the third or fourth time, so they stuck him away."

Dudley was a lot more lucid than I thought he would be. This seemed like a great lead.

"You sure his name is Karl Hackney?"

"Yeah, pretty sure. When he moved in with Rhonda, everyone else had to back off her. He's a mean dude. Tried to kill a guy once for scratching his bike.

Did time for that too."

Dudley went on to describe Karl is less than complimentary terms, at one point calling him an animal, which I thought was interesting coming from someone who lives in a park.

"OK, Dudley. Appreciate your help." I had a fifty rolled up in my jacket pocket and slipped it to him. He palmed the money like he was picking up a baby sparrow.

"Anytime. You know where to find me." As I walked away, I saw Dudley pull himself off the bench and shuffle towards the liquor store.

I chewed on this on the drive back into the city. If it is common knowledge that the guy Karl was Rhonda's main squeeze, it makes sense that he is a primary suspect in the fathering. And, if he got put away, it also makes sense that Rhonda is looking around for another meal ticket and saw Doc standing there like a Salvation Army poster.

When I got back to the office, I found a message from Mary Ann waiting for me. I figured I would keep what progress I had made quiet until I knew more. I called her at work and found she had called in sick. I tried her at home and found her slightly hysterical.

"Oh my God, they've threatened to kill Doc!"

"Who, and, for God's sake, why?"

"He's really scared. I guess an old boyfriend had a lot of stuff in Ronda's house. So, they had a yard sale and sold it. Next thing, a call comes in from some guy who says he's the brother of the guy that owned the stuff and that, when his brother gets out of jail, he wants the stuff. Doc told him it's gone and the guy said his brother would come to get it. If it wasn't there he would "take care" of Doc."

"What did Doc say?"

"He told me he told the guy to tell his brother to go fuck himself. But, I don't think Doc is really that tough."

I'm thinking, not a good idea to play tough guy with what I hear about Karl, especially when you're not much more than five feet tall. Now it turns out that there is also has a brother in his corner, so Doc is already not only out weighed, he's out numbered.

"What's Doc going to do?"

"Nothing I guess. I'm afraid Doc will say or do something that will get these guys really mad at him."

It was time to tell her about Karl. "Mary Ann, the guy in jail was Rhonda's live-in boyfriend. I have to follow up on him, but I don't think it's wise for Doc to aggravate the situation. Can he get any of the stuff back?"

"I don't think so. It was a bunch of motorcycle parts and stuff. Doc sold it and spent the money."

"Tell Doc to keep his head down and stop yanking on the gorilla. Maybe I can do something."

I decided to do some research on Karl to see what I was dealing with. I ran his criminal records and found he had been convicted of assault and battery (one year probation), breaking and entering (suspended sentence), assault and battery with a deadly weapon (eighteen months, house of correction) and breaking and entering (two years, house of correction). A busy biker. I made more phone calls over two days and finally found another classmate who remembered Rhonda and Karl. According to him, Rhonda went down more than the chairs on the Titanic, hinting that he was one of the chairs. Most of that seemed to stop after Karl hooked up with her. Probably not because Rhonda lost her appetite, but probably more so because Karl was so scary. I checked Department of Corrections and found Karl incarcerated in Norfolk House of Correction, a medium security facility south of the city. He was serving a two year sentence and was eligible for parole in two months. I had to pay him a visit.

Norfolk House of Correction looms like a malevolent barge, beached in the woods. The town of Norfolk is only forty minutes away in distance, but a generation away in attitude. People drive slowly and often honk at their friends when they pass. There are no chain fast food restaurants, but still silver diners featuring "home made" food. But once through the town you are jarred by the imposing winter-gray prison. I got the impression the town folks have gotten to a point where it's invisible and ignored, but it still sits with a lonely hue around it.

I had called ahead and was assured Karl was still there and would accept a visitor. I figured his calendar was not too crowded and I made an appointment for eleven in the morning. No matter how many times you visit a house of correction, the sense of dread folds over you like a wet woolen blanket. Norfolk Prison sat squat and gray like a predatory reptile. There is no joy in its aura.

I signed in, was identified, searched and given a list of don'ts. There were no dos. I was ushered through a metal detector and led into the visitor's room. It too was gray with cubicles for talking. I was the only civilian in the room. I guess the inmates aren't too popular.

After couple of minutes, a guard led in Karl. He was large and scary, as described. He wore a dark green tee shirt with the short sleeves cut off. Each arm was tattooed with the standards. His gut looked flat and he was solid all around, thanks to the prison weight room. His hair was balding on top, but the back was long to his shoulders. He could fit right in with any biker gang in the country. He was smiling like a cobra as he sat down.

"Don't know if I ever met a PI," he said, his voice higher than you would expect.

"Not like TV, huh?"

He gave me a grin. I liked him.

"Who knows? Just like here, the world is full of different kinds. What do you want?" The smile was gone and his eyes had gone hard.

"This is kind of whacky. There is a little guy, Doc, who thinks he is the father of Rhonda's son. I don't think he is. In fact, I think you are."

His face morphed into a laugh that was not nice. "I know who that little shit is. He sold my stuff. When I get out of here, I'm going to turn him inside out." He quickly looked around to see who heard him. Not a good idea to make threats while hoping for parole.

"I heard. I figure he's not the brightest bulb."

"That fuckin Rhonda." Now he lowered his voice. "I'll deal with her too."

"Frankly, Karl, I don't care, although if I was asked, I'd say I was on your side."

"Rhonda was a good squeeze part of the time. The rest of the time she was a bitch. I had to keep an eye on her because every asshole on the North Shore was lookin to get a piece of that."

"Well, she's got Doc living with her because she says Doc is the father. He's too stupid to know one way or the other. What's the real story?"

"The rug rat's mine. At least he better be. Last time I looked, he even looked like me. I was thinking the other night that it might be good to see him again and maybe have him hang with me."

"Fatherhood's a beautiful thing." I hoped I didn't sound too sarcastic.

"Yeah." If Karl could get wistful, this was probably as close as he would get.

"So, the kid's not Doc's, for sure."

"Yeah, that's right. That little shit better clear out before I get out."

"When is that going to be?"

"I'm up for review in two months. Might get out then, but doesn't look that good. Some behavior shit and no job that I know of and Rhonda's got to vouch for me and she won't even talk to them. She wants me to sit here forever so she can fuck around and sell my shit. If they pass on me then, I got another year or so. I can't go that long knowing that shit Doc is out there grazing in my grass."

"So, how's the story work out?"

"I met Rhonda at the Rusty Rudder a long time

ago. First night we went behind the bar and fucked like rabbits. After a couple of months, I ran into her again, just before I went away. I stayed with her for a little while, then did a year. She came in for me and I got out early. That's when I moved in with her. Pretty soon she gets knocked up and has the boy. I'm movin' with some bro's at the time and wasn't around much. Went out to the Coast and shit. Came back and moved back in with her. She acted like she couldn't get enough of me at first, then I heard she was fuckin around again. Caught one asshole in the house and beat the shit out of him. Didn't seem to faze her though."

"So you need her to vouch for you at the parole board to get out early?"

"This is the second time. The first time I came up she didn't show. I heard they called her and she said to leave me in here. I'll take care of her too when I get out."

I could see Karl had a fuse as short as a Vermont summer. I could see his neck pump up as he talked. "What's your chances without her?" I asked.

He looked around briefly as he lost concentration. "What?"

"I was wondering how tough it will be for you if Rhonda doesn't stand up."

"Not fuckin good. But I still will try so I can settle some scores. Especially with that little shit Doc." He settled back in his chair, gave me a dead eye stare, and then grinned. He was a man with a mission.

"You mind if I explain to my client that you're the father and get Doc out of there?"

"Nah. It's the truth. I never lie. And, maybe

I'll be a better old man to the kid. Doc can't do shit, especially make a kid with Rhonda. He would be lucky to get it up with her. Do what you want to do."

We smiled at each other. I understood Karl had his code of ethics that might vary with the accepted norm, but worked for him. I didn't doubt for a second that he was truthful in both what he said and what he said was going to do. I figured Doc was in a world of bad trouble.

We both stood up with a small smattering of mutual respect. He wasn't that much bigger than me, but he seemed to take up much more space. Maybe we could have a beer together.

I was back in my office in an hour. I put my feet up and stared out the window at the traffic crawling along. Didn't seem much point in going further. I believed Karl and it made sense he was the father. Doc was just a stupid stooge and meal ticket for Rhonda. He really was a clown. I wondered how many lives were mixed in badly with hers. I pulled together all my notes and started with the final report. Three hours later I was finished. I detailed all that I did and it came out to about thirty five pages. I gave it to Rachel to bind up at Kinko's and called Mary Ann. She answered on the second ring.

"I think we should meet, Mary Ann. I want to get you up to date. I think you will find it interesting."

"Do you know Doc's innocent?"

"I don't think I would use those words, but, yes, you will probably like the results."

We made an appointment in the huge Chinese restaurant on Route One for six o'clock the next day, right after she got out of work. The Kowloon is a looming faux pagoda trying to look like an Oriental fantasy, but comes off as a combination of a Hollywood set and a wholesale club. I got there twenty minutes early and sat at a booth with a view of the front entrance. I ordered a couple of appetizers and waited. Mary Ann came in ten minutes later. Her cotton dress came down below here knees and she had on a white cardigan sweater, buttoned up. I waved and she came over without a smile.

"Hi," I said. "I've got some appetizers coming. Care for a glass of wine?"

"That would be nice." She was very nervous. "I like white Zinfandel."

I signaled to the waiter and ordered the wine for her and a Kettle One vodka martini for me. I waited for the drinks to show up before I started.

"Well, I have a report for you. Before I give it to you, I'll summarize the situation."

She took a small sip, looking down into the glass with beagle eyes.

"Mary Ann, you're right. Doc is not the father. I believe Rhonda lied to him so she would have someone with her, either as a companion or for extra financial support." She took another sip, and looked up at me. I could see tears weal up. "Tell me about it." Her voice was small and thin.

"Rhonda has had a lot of lovers, but years ago, she took up with a guy by the name of Karl Hackney. He moved in with her and lived with her off and on for three or four years. The little boy is his, not Doc's."

"What happened to him?"

"Hackney's in prison. Not the first time. He's a

biker and rather nasty. The last time he went in, he and Rhonda were on the outs, mainly because he paid little attention to her or the boy, except to maintain a type of ownership over her. I gather she is glad he's in the slammer."

Mary Ann's shoulders sank slightly. "Oh God, thank you. Can I tell Doc?"

"Mary Ann, you can tell Doc because it's the truth. But, also tell Doc he should get as far away from Rhonda as he can. You too."

"Why?"

"Doc seems to have upset Karl to a point where I think it's dangerous for him. He and Rhonda sold Karl's biker equipment in a yard sale. Karl got wind of it and Doc gave his brother a hard time on the phone. Karl swears he is going to "take care" of Doc when he gets out. I wouldn't cancel Rhonda's insurance either."

She was looking at the bound report I had under my arm on the table. "I don't understand."

I figured there was a lot Mary Ann didn't understand. I slid the report over to her.

"Mary Ann, you are a nice person. These people are not nice people. My advice is to take this report home, read it twice, have a good cry and get as far away from Doc and Rhonda as you can. Chalk it up to one of life's regrets, and don't get tangled up more than you already are."

She pulled the report over like it was going to bite her. She opened the first page, glanced at it and sighed. The tears were more obvious now.

I sent my bill and was pleasantly surprised to

receive payment in full within a week. I gave it little thought until Mary Ann's call ten months later.

"Dan, I need you. It's horrible." Her voice was soft and scratchy.

"Mary Ann, you didn't get caught up with Doc again. Did you?"

"I read your report and thought about Karl and how he was a victim like me." I had trouble visualizing Karl as a victim instead of the victimizer.

"Anyway, I went to the prison to visit him and we seemed like soul mates. He said he was coming up for parole and needed a sponsor. So I went in and said I would do that and even would find a job for him. So, they let him out and he moved in with me."

I sighed. "Mary Ann, you had Karl move in with you? Did he get involved with Doc and Rhonda again?"

"No, he was wonderful. He had some words with Doc, and I think Doc was scared and he disappeared for a while. I was in love with Karl."

"What do you mean, was?"

"That's why I need you. Karl was killed on his motorcycle two weeks ago. I'm sure Doc had something to do with it, like cut his brakes or something. Please help me prove it."

Mary Ann was determined to be a loser. "I don't know, Mary Ann. You're alleging murder. Have you talked to the police?"

"I did and they don't seem to want to do anything. I don't think they liked Karl." I figured that was an understatement. "I've got what's left of his motorcycle in my garage. Just come and look at it.

Please."

"OK, I'll look at it and you can tell me more. I'll be over today at six o'clock."

Mary Ann's house was a peeling small Cape in a lower middle class neighbor hood. There were pale blue shutters, one of them sagging, on the two front windows. Most of the houses on the street exuded struggle. The garage door was closed when I arrived.

She came to the door wearing a baggy sweat suit. Under her eyes was charcoal smeared and she looked ten years older from when I last saw her. She offered coffee and I took it and sat with her at a maple dining table with only two chairs in the kitchen. It smelled of burnt cheese.

"OK, tell me what happened."

"Like I said, I went to the prison. I had to be sure Doc was not the father. Karl and I talked for about an hour and we started writing. He was really a wonderful man and hardly anyone understood him. His parole came up two months later and I went in. I told the board that I would sponsor him. I kind of lied and told them I had known him for some years. Anyway, they let him out into my custody. He moved right in and it was wonderful."

"So, let me figure this out. You were looking to get Doc back, but got Karl, the real father instead."

"Well, Karl's really more of a man than Doc. Karl was going to beat up Doc for selling his biker stuff, but I asked him not to. Doc's still with Rhonda and I think Karl was happy with that. But Doc was still scared and I think he fixed Karl's bike so he crashed. Oh, my

God, it's so awful!" She started to shake and some tears welled up. As goofy as she was at wrecking her life, I liked her and felt bad for her. This was a woman who, although couldn't help doing bad things to herself, was not catching any breaks. I sipped at my coffee, gave her a quiet minute, then said, "Let's take a look at the bike."

It took a minute for her to settle down, and, when she did, we went through a side door into the attached single car garage. There were a couple of boxes of clothes and household junk, but most of the garage was taken with what was left of Karl's Harley. It was really a pile of bent and broken pieces, most of which were in a wicker basket. The frame was recognizable, but was seriously bent. He had hit something head on which pushed the front fork back into the engine cavity.

Pipes and fenders were strewn across the side of the garage. I suspected there were some pieces missing, probably some missing from Karl as well. He went out with a flourish.

"OK, Mary Ann, I'll take a look, but there is any hint of foul play, I'm getting the cops involved."

"Thank you, Bob. I need some piece of mind. I just don't what to do and now I'm scared of Doc."

Karl was extinguished forty minutes west of the city in the town of Billerica. I went to the Billerica police station and talked to the chief there. He was mildly bemused I was looking at this and I could tell his only regret was that Karl met his maker in his jurisdiction because of the paperwork he had to fill out. But, he gave me a copy of the police report which gave me the location, and time. Apparently Karl went pretty much head on into a car full of Fort Devons troopers. I had names and knew they were billeted on the fort. I then drove out to the scene.

It was a pretty New England two lane, undulating and curving around occasional Capes and farm stands. Where Karl met his demise was the crest of a rolling hill, with large maple trees on either side, and a culvert on the right. I got out of my car and walked along the shoulder. There was no sign any thing catastrophic had occurred there. Birds could be heard and traffic was as light as a Sunday morning. The road was no doubt initially built when cars traveled at a respectable thirty five. A motorcycle rocketing at more than sixty miles an hour would have a hard time holding onto the pavement. The police report estimated Karl was sailing along at about seventy. Living on the edge, that Karl.

I got back in my car and drove five miles in one direction, and then five miles back again in the other. There were four bars in that ten mile stretch and I stopped in each. All were tired and smelled of stale beer and hard times. Three bartenders did not remember Karl, but the guy in Junior's, did. He carried a large gut that hung over his belt and had tattoos up each arm. He was fashionably dressed in Farmer John overalls with a Harley Davidson tee shirt underneath. He was totally unimpressed to meet a private eye.

"I remember that asshole. He rolled in here pretty shitfaced, drank three or four shooters and tried to pick up the waitress. I figured when he took off, he was headed for trouble. Most bikers know when to stop. He said he was stopping in every place he came to, looking for pussy. Had to be one crazy skank to go with that asshole."

"Pretty drunk?"

"I had to cut him off. Know how hard that is to happen in this place? He was fuckin wasted."

I decided I didn't have to continue my bar surveys any further. I headed over to Fort Devons. It took a while to get through the front gate and into the mess hall, where they said at least one of the troopers would meet me. I sat at a long wooden table infused with old grease for about twenty minutes when a young clean cut looking guy in fatigues came in. As I was the only one in a blue blazer with a black tee shirt underneath, it wasn't hard for him to figure out I was the one to see.

His name was PFC Andrew Collins and he was the kind of man that makes you proud. In shape, polite and brimming with integrity, we drank coffee and chatted about the military, being homesick and the sorry state of our politicians. On that night he was riding shotgun in a car with three other troopers. They were on their way for a beer or two, nothing much different from any other time they could get off the fort. From what I knew, and what happened to him, we pieced together what happened to Karl that night. It was about 10:30 and the four soldiers were in a blue Buick sedan, going for beer and pizza. They were traveling about forty miles an hour without a car in sight. Karl apparently was motoring like a demon from hell towards them in the other direction. I was pretty sure he was drunk and traveling, as they say, in excess. Further, Karl, cresting the hill, at about seventy miles an hour, happened to be on the wrong side of the road, surprising the hell out of the guys in the Buick. But instead of swerving to his right, Karl turned his bike to the left shoulder, trying to pass the car on its right. He may have made it if it wasn't for the culvert. He hit that unmovable chunk of cement at high speed launching him over the handlebars, like some kind of out of control superhero.

PFC Collins said, "The thing I remember was this guy flying at us head first. He had this incredible grin on his face and hit up right by the hood ornament. Then he rolled underneath and was gone and the car made a big bump. It was sickening."

"You guys stop right away?"

"Yeah, we all jumped out. He was laying in a lump way back on the shoulder. The bike, or whatever was left of it, had gone sailing into the field. It didn't take a medic to know that guy was gone. Bill, one of the guys, puked right on the spot. It was horrible."

"How long for the cops to get there."

"We called right away and they showed up with an ambulance about twenty minutes later. We all gave statements, but they didn't seem too interested. Sort of routine."

I shook hands with PFC Collins and made my way back to Boston.

I put together another report; this one about fifteen pages long and called Mary Ann. We met in the same dark Chinese restaurant, and had the same chicken fingers and egg rolls. I bought a Mai Tai for her and a martini for me. I figured we both could use them. After the first two sips and after she pulled the paper umbrella out of her glass, I handed her the second report.

"Here it is, Mary Ann. Doc had nothing to do with Karl's demise. Karl had everything to do with his demise. It was inevitable. I suggest you go home, read this and have a good cry. Then think about looking around for different choices."

She was teary. Her face and jaw sagged and she seemed years older. There was a film over her eyes. I slid the report closer to her and she looked at it like it was a dangerous creature. After a minute she picked it up and placed it into her vinyl bag.

"Thank you, Dan. I feel so lost."

I could tell she wanted me to take her someplace. Her sorrow seemed to seep deep into her being, and she needed something like physical human relations to make her feel alive again. I could not wait to get away.

"Mary Ann, there is nothing more I can do for you. The best of luck in the future," I said softly. We were quiet for a minute and I patted her on the hand and slid out of the booth, leaving her staring into her drink glass. I walked into the parking lot and slowly drove away, watching in the mirror to see if she came out. I never heard from her again.

MARRIED PEOPLE ARE CRAZY
Sometimes you do bad to make good.

I made the mistake of appearing on a morning television show, the kind that only people who do not work and have not much else to do, watch. It was as bland as oatmeal. The host thought housewives would love to see two private investigators, and scheduled me and a hot female private detective.

I, of course, was fairly typical, taking about surveillances, video and interrogations. My co-guest offered specialized service to wives in which she flirted and tempted their husbands to see if they would entertain the idea of being unfaithful. This femme fatale was very attractive, very nicely endowed top and bottom, and bought her clothes at the escort service boutique. Even on TV, her nipples were sitting up. No mystery as to her success, as the male species is as weak as overcooked oatmeal. Almost every husband she tempted rolled over like a dog in heat, and the wives said that they suspected it all along, and paid her ridiculous bills.

About a week later, I got a call from a woman who said her friend had seen me on the program and asked me to meet them both. We made an appointment to meet in a Denny's on the North Shore at two o'clock, the next day.

I got there twenty minutes early and slid into a purple vinyl booth with a view of the front parking area. A waitress, who looked like her feet hurt, came over after a minute and asked if I wanted breakfast. I ordered black coffee and watched the traffic streaming into the mall across the road. Right on time, a heavy grey Mercedes parked in front. Inside I could see two middle-aged women wearing enormous black sunglasses inside. They sat there for a couple of minutes, unsure. When they got out of the car, the younger of the two came around to the driver's side and they talked for a minute. I figured her for the "friend" and the driver and possibly my new client. The "friend" was a fairly trim late fifties-something, wearing too blue slacks and a flowered blouse, cut low. The driver was decked out in Talbot's Woman, thick at the waist with low heeled shoes. They came in together, stopped at the door and searched the restaurant. They gave a look of recognition as they saw me, the result of my television exposure. The friend led the way and they sat together opposite me. The tired waitress took their order for two iced teas as they scrutinized my business card. The friend introduced herself as Jill and introduced the driver as Betty. It was clear who pushed this meeting.

"How can I help?"

Jill said, "Well, it's really not for me. It's for Betty, but I will help as much as possible."

"OK, Betty, "turning towards her, "how can I help?'

"I saw you on TV and thought maybe you were different." Her voice was soft and polite, like a stranger asking directions in a strange country. "I've been going through a divorce. It's been going on now for almost three years."

No surprise so far. "Who do you think I'm

different from?"

"I'm sure my husband has been having an affair with his secretary. I've hired three different detectives and no one can catch him."

"Why do you think he's having an affair? And, don't forget this is a no fault state, adultery doesn't matter."

"My husband, Bill. That's his name, Bill, made a lot of money. He was in waste management and sold the company about six years ago. But, he still rented a small office and kept the same secretary, even though he really doesn't have a business anymore."

"Again, Betty, the information you are looking for may not be of any help with your divorce."

"I know. But, I have to know and want to catch him; my lawyer says that if we can show how I am victimized, it will be helpful."

"How long has this been going on?"

She sighed, and took a sip of her ice tea. "The divorce has been going on for almost three years. We were married for thirty three years. I never worked, just took care of him and the kids."

"Is there a custody issue with the kids?"

"No, they're grown. I just want what's fair."

Jill jumped in. "He's a bastard. Betty gave him all of the best of her years and he just screws around and drinks."

Betty looked at her sharply. "Bill's a recovering alcoholic. He works hard at staying sober. But, I can't forgive him with this secretary of his."

"So, you want him followed to get evidence he is

cheating with his secretary?"

"I've hired three different detectives to do that and none of them can catch him. He's really sneaky," she said.

"If they can't catch him, maybe he's not doing it, "I said.

Jill piped in again, "He's doing it all right, he just sees them and they lose him. Betty's right, he's really sneaky."

They both seemed anxious. I said, "Surveillance is surveillance. Some are good at it, most are terrible. But if you've had three different people try to tail your husband with no success, he's probably pretty adept at counter surveillance techniques. I think I'm pretty good, but if someone wants to blow off a tail, it's the easiest thing in the world to do."

Betty turned to Jill,"See I told you there was nothing more I can do. He always wins. All my life I've been giving and giving and I'll have nothing to show for it." Her voice was weak and low.

We were quiet for a moment. Jill took a sip of her ice tea and said,"Look, my friend is hurting and that SOB continues to rub it in her face. There must be something you can do." Betty looked at me expectantly.

I thought for a minute. "Are you two now separated?"

Betty answered, "I'm still in the big house in Beverly Farms. He's been living in the beach house. He still has a lot of his clothes and stuff in the big house."

"Do you have legitimate access to the beach house?"

"I guess so. I still have the keys, but I never hardly go there."

We sat still for a minute, and I said, "OK, let me think about this and see if I can come up with any ideas. Give me all your info and I'll call you back in a day or so."

I sat in my office, watching girls in short skirts on Boylston Street out my second floor window. I ran a background on Betty and Bill. He was in waste management, selling his company for big bucks five years ago. He had the usual variety of civil suits against him, and seemed like he played pretty fast and loose throughout his business life... Betty was almost non-existent, obviously being what she said she was, a dutiful housewife, making beds and cooking and out of the loop of Bill's world. I called her and made arrangements to meet her at the beach house the next afternoon, when she knew Bill would be elsewhere.

Beaches on the north shore of Boston can be almost primal in their beauty. Often with tall grassy dunes, and rocky inlets, the scenery makes up for the frigid waters. This beach house was in one such place. I drove down a narrow winding road, with wet lands on one side, and scrub pines on the other. Birds of all kinds seemed to command the area, gliding like kites over the rolling dunes. The house, an angular contemporary of cedar and glass came into view as I rounded the final curve. It sat inside high sand, overlooking the white capped studded Atlantic. Betty's Mercedes was already parked there.

She let me into a vaulted ceiling living room,

dominated by a salt spray coated floor to ceiling window. There was a look of eagerness in her eyes, but she was obviously uneasy in her husband's lair. I smiled, "Hi Betty, anything new develop?"

"No," she said, "still the same. The lawyers talk to each other and I have no idea what about. God, I hope you can help me."

"OK, Betty," I said. "Here's the deal." I opened my briefcase and brought out a black plastic box. "You can stick this onto a phone jack, and it will record conversations both ways, whenever some calls out or in. I will give this to you and show you how it works. I'll send you a generic bill, sell it to you, and you can do whatever you want, but, I'll warn you, you shouldn't."

Betty looked at it like it was a living insect. "How does it work?"

I looked around and found a phone jack behind a large horizontal oak credenza. I grabbed one end and pulled it away from the wall. The jack was occupied by a phone ten feet away. I plugged in a line splitter and then the device.

"This has a voice activated tape recorder. Whenever the phone is used in the house, regardless of which extension, the recorder will turn on. You will have to come in from time to time to change tapes if you decide to use this. But, I want to tell you, this is not exactly kosher. I will give you this and you can decide for yourself. I don't want to know from nothing. That's all I can do for you and, frankly, I don't recommend it." I pushed the credenza back into place.

"I don't know what I'll do, but thank you for the

help," she said.

"OK, Betty. Good luck. I don't expect to see you again."

I left her standing on a red and blue Oriental rug that probably cost more than my car, staring at the credenza. I felt her confusion and was sad for her.

I didn't hear anything for two weeks. I sent a bill for services rendered and got a check back in three days. Then she called.

"Dan, it's fantastic," she said. "He's talking to her all the time, making dates and everything. I really know now what's going on."

"I really don't want to know, but I'm glad it's working out for you."

"I'm a little surprised that it kind of sounds sort of innocent, but it still answers a lot of questions for me." She was ecstatic.

Betty, you know that none of that can be used, "I cautioned.

"I know, I know. But, thank you."

I got another similar call, and then another one I was seriously thinking about not taking, but I did. This time her voice was shaky and worried.

"Dan, I think I did a bad thing."

My stomach flipped. "What did you do, Betty?"

"Well, I called in for another deposition by my husband's attorneys. He got a bunch of them. All of them cost a lot of money."

"And?"

"Well, one of them asked me if I had every hired a detective to follow my husband and I said yes." Then, later on, he asked me if I had ever bugged my husband's phones and I said yes again. He seemed to be very interested in that."

"And?" I asked softly.

"He asked me what private investigator was involved and I told him you and your agency. I think that was wrong."

I felt my pulse accelerate like a rocket. I said nothing for several seconds, as I pondered her I.Q.

Then she asked, "Did I do wrong?"

"You could say that. Betty, listen to me. Go to the beach house, get that equipment and throw it as far into the ocean that you can. Then forget about me and or anything you asked me to do."

"OK, Dan. I'll do it right away. I'm really sorry."

For the next two hours, I had visions of putting my hand up in front of a battery of bloodthirsty lawyers in two thousand dollar suits. Then she called back again.

"You won't believe what happened," she blurted.

I had a small heart fibulas ion. "What happened, now, Betty?"

"Well, I went right up to the beach house, like you said. I was trying to pull the credenza away from the wall, but you know how heavy it is and I was having a hard time. Anyway, as I was pulling, I felt someone behind me. I knew right away it was Bill."

"So he caught you with the stuff."

"Not exactly. But, now that I knew all the things he was up to, I felt somehow stronger. So, I got mad and I turned around and said that I bugged his phones and knew everything." He just looked at me for a minute, then he said that he knew. Then he said that he never thought I would have the courage to do anything like that. He said he didn't realize how strong I could be. He said that he saw me differently."

"He saw you differently?" I had a hard time envisioning the situation.

"Yes, he said he was misjudging me. He said he thought I was weak. He said he saw that I am tougher than he thought. He said he realized I was not just a housewife. We talked for a while, and then we hugged and even kissed. I haven't felt that way about Bill in a long time. Anyway, he says we should call off the divorce and try to reconcile."

"Betty, are you telling me that everything has changed because of what you did?"

"It's unbelievable. Bill's going to call the lawyers tomorrow. He's moving back into the big house with me. Thank you, thank you."

I let out a deep breath. "I'm glad it's worked out. Did you get rid of the equipment?"

"I did what you said." She exclaimed, then, "It's so wonderful. Thank you so much."

"OK, I said. "You go and have a great life and good luck."

I hung up and stared out the window without seeing anything. There is no accounting for the behavior of the human race.

A little more than a year later, Betty called again. "Dan, I need you."

"No you don't."

TROUBLE ON THE MOUNTAIN
Guests only see the surface.

It was a three hour drive, but I had a Nissan Z at the time and loved driving it. It was early spring and tiny green buds were just starting to appear on the trees under the warming sun. I crossed the Hudson River and picked up a pretty two lane for three or four miles before turning left at the impressive sign. A steep drive led up from the valley, s-turned, snaking for a half mile, passing under a gate house and finally leveling out into a broad parking lot with the hotel looming over like a Gothic cathedral. A dowager queen, it showed its age with dignity but obvious make-up. The resort perched on several thousand acres on top of a mountain in upstate New York. They bragged that on a clear day, you could see four states. On the upper floors, balconies hung off the building like iron perches, overlooking the Hudson valley on one side, and a clear Alpine lake on the other.

I met Don, an old client, in his office on the second floor. He smiled, held out his hand and stretched his long frame behind a Queen Anne desk. There was a spectacular view of forests and mountain trails from the window behind him. He was wearing a blue blazer over a white shirt and grey flannel slacks. The blazer had a gold crest on it the size of a cup saucer. Even though it was April, he sported a Hawaiian tropic tan.

"Dan, good to see you again." He said, welcoming.

"Good to see you. Looks like things are charging right along for you. This place is very impressive."

"Yes," he mused. "But like an antique car, it can look good from the outside, with rust and grime on the inside."

"I guess there is something wrong, because you called me here. An occupational hazard, people only call me when there is something to fix."

"Coffee?" He asked, and then called down for some. It arrived with a waiter almost immediately. "This place is privately owned and has been losing money for some time. A lot of money. They brought me in on a short contract to see what I could do."

I took a sip of coffee and waited.

"I crunched the numbers and saw that cost percentages are way out of line. There has to be some rats in the woodpile."

"In food and beverage mostly?" I asked.

"There, in supplies and you name it. Almost all of the help live on the property. We provide housing and have an employee dining room. We have trouble finding good people."

"Are they mostly local?"

"Some are, but we recruit all over the place. Hard to tell who's good or bad."

I thought about it for a minute. "Don. I could come in as a mystery guest all summer long and probably only scratch the surface on a property this big. Still might not be a bad idea, but I think you would get better insight with an undercover operative. Take an X-ray from the inside for you."

He thought for a minute. "I think that's a good idea. We get people from all over the place. Wouldn't be hard to slide in a plant to see what's going on."

"I take it the hiring season has started. I have a couple of guys working for me that would fit and may like doing it."

"We'll supply housing in the dorms and they eat in the employee cafeteria. What can your people do?"

"One guy has kitchen experience; the other has been in a couple of warehouse assignments. He could work in maintenance or something like that."

"You decide. Get me a good guy. I have to figure out what is going on here, and fast. I have a short contract with these guys."

"I'll work it out on my end and get back to you within a week. I'm going to roam around a little to get a feel for the property and head out. Thanks for the coffee and the business."

"Always a pleasure." He said as he uncoiled himself from behind the desk and shook my hand again. It was nice there was no mention of fees.

I headed out and down to the lobby, smiling at the attractive gal working at the desk. She smiled back. I wandered down a hallway fifteen feet wide, decorated with black and white photos of elegant times past, like distant shadows, to the dining room. Along the way, I passed libraries and lounges, all with heavy leather furniture and dark wood paneled walls. The dining room turned out to be cavernous, with a fireplace on one end large enough to stand inside. Leaded windows bowed out on the left side, looking out to a swimming pool and cabanas. There was easily fifty tables, all set with sparkling crystal and silver. It was like the Titanic had risen and beached itself on this mountain top.

Back in Boston, I called in Ted, who was just finishing an assignment as a sous chef in a local restaurant, ferreting out a drug dealer who was incidentally stealing shrimp and lobsters. Ted Wollaston was a beefy guy in his early twenties who loved beer and always had his baseball cap on backwards. He looked like he was on parole. That, plus a deceiving intelligence, made him a great undercover guy. He piled into my office and slung himself down in the guest chair, looping one leg over the arm. He was chewing gum, smelled of Budweiser, and grinned at me.

"What's up, boss?" He asked.

"Ted, how would you like to work at a five star resort this summer? You'd have to live on the property, eat there and hang around with the staff."

"Let's see. I would work at a resort, live and eat for free and get paid to do what I do?"

"This place has mucho problems. Almost everywhere you look. I need you to find the bad guys."

"How about chicks? Are there women there?"

"Tons. Hanging out and looking for summer love."

"What are the hours? Will I have time to party?"

"Are you kidding? The party never stops. The question is will you have time to work?"

"Sign me up. I'm there." He grinned like the Marquis de Sade at the Playboy mansion.

I drove back out the next day and sat down with Don. He was in a double breasted blazer with a soft white shirt and a lavender Hermes tie. Perfect for greeting incoming guests or critiquing the croquet matches.

"I've lined up one of my undercover investigators. He has kitchen experience and can be a waiter, as well. He's a big guy and can also fit in at maintenance. He's ready to go."

Don said, "I'm bringing in a group from Palm Springs. He can show up at the same time and roll in with everybody else. How does it work?"

"He's responsible to do a report everyday. He forwards them to me and I put it all together for weekly summaries. I work out the logistics and we backstop his background. But, don't forget, Don, nobody knows."

"I'm the only one, but let's work closely on this. The owners are old fashioned and very hinky about my methods. They have no idea what trouble this place is in."

I cruised back through western Connecticut to the office and gave Ted final instructions the next day and sent him away the next week. Sure enough, he was hired on the spot and moved into the employee dorms with no one the wiser. If he could keep his head screwed on straight, he would have one interesting summer.

Within the two weeks, Ted was cooking. One group that was hired for dining room help brought along enough grass and coke to fuel a 70's disco. Identifying the source was not hard as the dealer immediately pegged Ted as a doper and offered him a dime bag on the spot. Don checked and found the dealer's employment application was not quite right and let him go for falsification. Ted was earning his pay already. We had set up a code where if Ted got a message from his Aunt Irene, he was to call me two hours later from a secure location. He called on schedule and after three weeks, I set up a meeting to discuss the progress of the investigation. I drove out in an unseasonably warm day, with the top off the car, and met him in a friendly Friendly's, six miles up the road from the resort.

I arrived early and watched Ted stroll in with his ball cap still on backwards. He was wearing a Grateful Dead tee shirt and baggy shorts. He was already getting tanned so I figured he was not being overworked at the resort. He flopped down in the booth and immediately picked up the menu, searching for the largest hamburger available.

"So, how's it going, Ted?" I asked.

"Bacon, cheese double paddy melt, fires and a coke." He said. I called over the waitress.

"I take it the food is not so hot."

"It's fine when they steal it from the kitchen; sucks what they serve you at the mess hall. They seem to think that leftovers are best served all mushed together."

"So, stealing from the kitchen?"

"That's the least of it. I discovered they have an enormous marijuana garden in the woods. You should see the size of it. There will be enough dope for the staff and most of the guests and half of the town."

"They're growing dope on the property? You're not giving me enough in the reports. This is the first I heard of this garden." Disciplining undercover people is an exasperating art.

"Aw, Bob, give me a break. There is staff everywhere. And when I'm not working, there's a party going on. Where can I find a place to write, or even call?" I figured he had a point, but I had no sympathy.

"What else?"

"Dan, get another op in there. Every cash sale is going south and the maintenance guys seem to have a business on the side selling hotel tools and supplies."

"Let me guess; you have a suggestion."

"Well, my girlfriend would be great. There are a lot of couples up there and it would look natural."

"You are either highly dedicated or the local talent is not up to your standards."

He grinned at me and paused a minute. "I guess you could say both. The bimbos working there are all over me, but it gets old real quick. Talk about sloppy seconds. At the same time, another investigator would have a lot more access."

"I'll talk to Don about it. How's your cover?"

"They want me to be leader of the pack. There is no clue about what I really do."

I pondered the assignment as the waitress brought over his food. I ordered another coffee. "OK, steady as she goes. We have time here. The goal is to identify as many bad guys as possible, clean house so they can make the place profitable. Be cool."

Ted wiped the grease flowing from his chin. "I'm as cool as it gets. Got to go soon. They swiped six lobsters from the cooler and there's a cook-out behind the dorm. I'm the cook."

I figured Ted's cover was fine and his head was still screwed on straight. I called Don, gave him and update and discussed the idea of a second, female investigator. He green lighted that on the spot and Aunt Irene placed another call to Ted.

Ted's girlfriend, Samantha, did part time work for us, so I knew she could do the job. After two hours orientation, she went home to pack and I gave Don a heads up on her name and when she would be making application. Ted thought they should have code names. He wanted Eagle for himself and wanted Swallow for Samantha. I didn't ask. This was turning out to be a serious investigation.

The summer continued on with reports from Ted and Sam coming in slow, but full of information. I got a call one morning from Ted. "Hey boss, how's it going?" He sounded pumped.

"Ted, where are you? Are you calling from someplace safe?" I asked, sipping my second cup of coffee.

"Yeah, I'm in town picking up some supplies for the chef." He started laughing. "Boss, you are going to love this. Know that apartment by the gate, over the driveway as you come in?"

"Yeah, you mean where the caretaker lives?"

"You got it boss. That caretaker's name is Stan Owlowski. I find out he worked for another property about five years ago. Seems like he had a problem with his boss, the manager. They were not getting along, always arguing and he was about to get fired. So, Stan, the man, invites the manager, some guy named Horton, to go hunting. Rumor has it he told Horton he had a great place to get a big buck deer. So, while on this hunting trip, poor Mr. Horton gets snuffed by Stan. A twelve gauge slug in the chest does him in. Stan says it was an accident, but they charged him with murder. Couldn't prove it and Stan walked. Supposedly also he stabbed some guy in a bar a while back, too, but no charges were made on that one. Everyone stays away from that guy, for obvious reasons."

I thought for a minute. Don had mentioned Owlowski during one of our meetings and I remember him saying Owlowski was an odd duck. I couldn't remember ever seeing him, and I figured a guy who had no compulsions about blowing away his boss, would not have warm and fuzzy feelings about an undercover spy in his domain. I asked Ted, "Do you come in contact with this guy?"

"Nah, not much. He stays by himself. Eats alone and disappears sometimes for a day or two. Guys say he goes into the woods and eats squirrels and berries every once in a while."

"Stay clear. No sense poking the bear. Remember to keep your cover. Watch your back."

I could hear him chuckling on the phone, "Not to worry, boss. I've got my ass covered. Eagle out." He hung up.

By late August, I had almost two hundred pages of reports from the Eagle and Swallow. I drove back to the resort on a day so hot, the air shimmered appliance white. I had the car open with the air conditioning on and wearing a Boston Red Sox hat to keep the sun from frying my brain. The tires hissed on the soft blacktop of the road. It was cooler when I turned up the road that snaked up the mountain, and I gave a furtive glance up to the apartment over the gate, where I knew Owlowski lived and was probably cleaning his guns and torturing small animals.

Don was leaning back in his wine colored leather chair, acres of green in the window behind him. He was in an off white linen suit with a pale beige shirt and matching tie, setting off his tan. He was like George Hamilton auditioning for a Bogart movie.

Once again, the coffee and ice tea setting appeared almost instantly. I settled in and sipped my coffee, all the time Don sat smiling at me. "Read the reports?" I asked. "Jesus. If the owners saw them, they'd close the place down and auction off the acreage." He said. "I've got to get rid of a lot of people before they raid the place for dope, a guest gets killed, we go broke, or all of the above."

"I agree. The inmates are; you know." I replied

"How many people would you say?" I could tell he didn't want to know.

"Well, you've got five people stealing from the kitchen, another three in maintenance getting kick backs and stealing supplies, at least six people gardening dope patches, not to mention three in room service having sex in guest rooms two or three times a week. I'd say, if you got rid of about a dozen of the hard core assholes, the rest would be scared enough to fall into line. Can you survive the rest of the summer losing that many?"

"Dan, I've got to cut expenses. The best way is to cut payroll. The best way to cut payroll is to terminate for cause so there is no unemployment insurance costs or wrongful terminations. If we can take out a dozen people, I may be able to salvage this summer and show a small profit."

"I could do that many interrogations, but I have to be careful. Some to the information only my investigators know, and I don't want to blow their cover."

"Let's do it. I have to let the owners know. So far I haven't told them about the undercover people. They will shit an entire law firm. I'll set it up. Can you get back here in a couple of days?"

"You tell me and I'll be here."

We both looked out at the grounds. Two women in short white skirts, with white tops and visors were playing tennis intensely. I could see their bare arms glisten, and they returned serves, their skirts flew up. Each was wearing white briefs underneath. Don smiled at me and I smiled back. "I hope none of these guests ever realize what goes on behind the scenes." He mused.

Two days later I was back in a tan summer weight suit with a white shirt and red striped tie for the meeting with the owners. I was brought into the conference room where sat five people reeking of old money and scorn. Under a withering gaze, I explained my credentials and methodology. They were aghast at the idea of spies inside, but were more horrified as to what I had found. It was clear they did not like the whole concept of internal investigations, but gave the go-ahead to Don to wrap it up.

This time, back in his office, instead of coffee, Don ordered up ice and a bottle of Jack Daniels. He poured two glasses and sipped his carefully. We were quiet for a couple of minutes. Finally I asked, "These people live here. How are we going to get them off the property? Not in my car."

"I don't know. Let me work at that. When can you move?"

"If we are going to do this, let's do it fast. Everyday I worry about my peoples' cover."

"OK, let's go on a Monday or Tuesday. I'll have a couple of days to prepare for the weekend."

"Let's shoot for Tuesday. I'll make up a list of people I can interrogate, and run it by you. If you agree, I'll do them one at a time and run them off the property. The good part is we know where they are."

I was back again on Monday. The heat wave continued and even the top of the mountain suffered from lack of breezes. This time I checked in as a guest. I had been careful to enter from the back each time I met with Don and didn't think anyone had seen me outside of the executive suites. I wore a lime green golf shirt and tan linen slacks, hoping to look like a vacationer without purpose. Don had made a reservation for me for a suite, and I made my way from the front desk to an upper floor. The room had a fireplace out of a Hansel and Gretel story book and a bed covered with a white lace canopy. French doors opened to a precarious tiny wrought iron balcony. Stepping out onto it, you could see the verdant New York and Connecticut woods stretching for miles; the Hudson a silver thread in the distance. No place to be without a close personal friend.

I settled in, spent an hour on the phone to the office and gathered the outlines of all the information developed over the past two months. I watched the orange glow of a huge setting sun, feeling very much alone. By seven thirty, I decided to try dinner and wander around. The dining room was busy with a generous wait staff buzzing around like honeybees. There were forty shaker style tables with high back chairs arranged throughout, with the enormous fireplace, cold and black at the far wall. Of the fifty or so diners, there was no one sitting alone.

I waited at the entrance podium for a minute until a blond and perky hostess approached. Her short skirt enhanced the tan in her legs. She gave me a smile. Then I noticed a flicker of coldness in her eye. Paranoia, always an occupational hazard, kicked in. I had a feeling my cover was not so good.

Dinner was an edgy affair, as I was now convinced the entire staff was staring at me. I was the only single guest and that didn't help my uneasiness. The grilled chicken with fresh snap peas and garlic mashed potatoes was excellent, but I didn't linger over coffee.

I peeked into the lounge, then decided against an after dinner drink as the hair on the back of my neck did not relax.

I returned to my room early, in an effort to hide. I went over my notes, and then read until midnight. In the morning, I didn't venture out, but ordered scrambled eggs with fresh biscuits and coffee from room service. By nine thirty, I had made my way, unnoticed to Don's office. He was wearing a pale yellow summer suit, with a sky blue shirt and pink tie. His dapperness couldn't his nervousness.

"I'm ready to go, Don." I said. "How are we working the logistics?"

He was nervous, while my adrenalin was starting to flow. I was feeling good.

"You can talk to them in the office behind the kitchen. It's private there. From what you told me, it will work for you."

"OK," I said. "I am going to try to get admissions and written statements. When and if I do, what do I do with them?"

With this, Don gave me his first smile of the morning. "I've arranged for two state police cruisers to stand by. If you get the goods on anyone that are from someplace else, the staties will drive them to the dorm to get their stuff, then downtown to the bus station where they will be asked to leave town. If they're local, the same thing, the cops take them to get their stuff, then to town with a warning not to come back."

I smiled back. "Don, they must owe you a lot to help like that."

"I just want to clean house and get rid of the bad guys. It sends a message."

"OK, here's my list of people I want to interview." I gave Don a list of fifteen people. A lot to interview in one day. He looked at it and nodded.

"I've arranged for my HR girl to round them up for you." He gave me her number and I headed for the office. I had arranged the order of people from the dirtiest, and weakest to the casual morons, who just should be fired, hoping to blame the first guys I interviewed for giving up the rest. There were hard-core thieves and druggies, including two that were cultivating the marijuana field in the woods, spending more time farming than working.

I set up the office so I looked in command and called for the first, not knowing what would happen. It turned out that I was suspected of being who I am and that worked to my advantage. I made noises about hidden cameras, surveillances and any other disinformation I could think of to protect the cover of my undercovers. Even so, when I called for Ted, so I could include him in with the bad guys, he came in ashen faced. I started my acting routine, raising my voice in case my phony questioning could be overheard. Ted whispered to me, "I've got two slashed tires on my car." They had smelled him out.

"What about Swallow?" I hushed to him.

"Nothing so far, but she's freaked."

"Ted, play this game, then get the hell out of here. Go with her and leave your car. I'll have the tires fixed and towed downtown. Just you two get. You never know. And stay away from Owlowski." He nodded and took off. I was hoping the look of fear on his face would be mistaken for guilt and there would be enough confusion for them to be able to take off. It became more and more apparent that the group we targeted was capable of hurting. I cranked up my game face.

When I was done, I had sixteen statements, including Ted's, with admissions from everything from swiping bottles from the bar, selling dope to guests to getting kickbacks from a couple of local vendors. The state police, grinning the whole time, ran them all off the property. I was finished by five o'clock and back in Don's office. His smile had turned to a huge grin.

"Dan," he said. "My job depended on you, today. The owners did not really believe it was as bad as it was. If you came up dry with the interviews, my head was on the chopping block. But, they're believers, now."

"Have you got people to fill in?" I asked, knowing that I'd seriously reduced his staff.

"Half of the people were worthless anyway, and we've got a half dozen good people lined up. I'm in good shape."

I took a deep breath. The adrenalin was wearing off. "Don, one thing I was not able to lock down is Owlowski. People are afraid of him. When I brought him up, I could see the fear quotient rise. I think that guy's dangerous."

"I agree, but no one will touch him for that reason. I'm hoping I can just keep him out in left field and away from everybody and everything, until I finish my contract." He shrugged.

I was anxious to get off the property. It was a very tense forty-eight hours. I stood up and shook hands with Don. It was the end of the day and he still looked like he stepped out of GQ.

"Send me the bill," he said.

"Not to worry," I replied.

The summer day was starting to wane with an early August stillness. There was a faint insect buzz from the woods and the humidity hung damp like a warm blanket. As I walked to my Z, I saw no one but felt a thousand eyes. The car was intact, except for a note on the windshield. It said, "Watch your back," in block letters.

    I started the car and sat for a minute to see if I could notice any movement. There was no one. I took my Smith and Wesson from the holster in the small of my back and laid it on the passenger seat. The first time I'd ever done that. Then I started the long road down the mountain, winding around rock outcrops and powerful pines, under Owlowski's apartment at the lower gate, and down into the valley and away. I locked the car on cruise at seventy miles an hour, headed for home and exhaled.

SORRY I DID IT EVEN ONCE
Some cases you should never do

Chestnut Hill is an enclave west of Boston comprised of huge leafy trees, large houses and money, old and new. I was driving there to meet a woman who said, in a clipped Yankee accent, she was desperate and had to see me immediately. I checked out the address through my reverse directory and found it was owned by a man very big in the retail business. This might be interesting.

It was late spring and, as I made my way through the light traffic, it seemed like I passed a landscaping truck every five houses. After one miss, I found the house, a grey stone Tudor, set back and up from the road. A driveway wound up on the left side of the house, and I could see a white Mercedes sport car and a grey Lincoln parked along side. I parked in front and walked up the walk to the oak front door, a slab as big as a pool table, with a wrought iron knocker, shaped like a lions head bolted to the middle. I banged it three times and waited.

Opening the door was a slender woman in her late thirties or very well preserved forties, dressed in a white silk blouse with black slacks. The blouse was opened three buttons down. There was no smile and before I could speak, she stood aside.

"You must be here for Natalie. She's in the parlor." She turned and walked deep into the dark and cool recesses of the house.

I stepped in and found another woman standing in the room just on the right. It was a masculine room with large deep red leather chairs and a stone fireplace. There was dark wood wainscoting and shelves of books lined the walls. This woman was wearing a cotton shift that came down to her practical shoes. The shift was buttoned to her neck. She was tense and obviously distraught. I put my hand out, "I'm Dan. You need some help?"

She was shaking as she held out her hand. "I'm Natalie. God, I hope you can help me." Her anxiety was palatable.

"What's the problem?"

"It's my son, Ed. Ronald ran off with him."

"Are you talking kidnapped?"

"Yes," she hissed. "He kidnapped Ed."

"And Ronald is who?" I was getting very worried about this situation. Over my shoulder I felt the door answerer standing. I glanced around and she gave me a look normally reserved for highway rest stops. I half turned and tried to give her my charming smile, but her expression did not change. She did speak, however. "Would anyone like coffee?" Her voice was like good scotch poured over ice.

"Yes, thank you." I then turned back to Natalie, who looked on the verge of tears.

"Tell me the whole story. Mind if I sit?"

I sat in an oversized maroon leather wing chair and Natalie primly positioned herself on the couch opposite. The door answerer unfortunately left, possibly to get the coffee.

Natalie took a deep breathe and started. "I was married to Ronald four years ago. He was awful, but somehow Ed came along."

"How old is Ed?" I asked.

"He's two now." She gazed for a second over my shoulder. "Anyway, Ronald and I are getting divorced. It's almost finished. It's cost Daddy a lot of money, but I am finally getting out."

I waited, letting her continue.

"We had a good arrangement worked out until the divorce is final. Ed would be with each of us every other weekend."

"Was there a formal custody arrangement?"

"You mean from the court? No, not yet, but we had agreed to share Ed's time."

She gazed over my shoulder again and I stayed quiet. The door answerer came in with a silver tray with coffee service in china cups. She placed the tray down in front of us, pleasantly bending over, then left without a word. I figured she must be the wife, but was easily twenty-five years younger than the owner of the property that I had researched.

Natalie continued in gasps. "Then two weeks ago, I dropped Ed off at where Ronald was staying. When I went back to pick him up, Ed and Ronald were gone. He ran off with him." She choked off a sob. "He kidnapped him!"

"Where do you think Ronald took him?"

"I don't know, but Ronald has family in the Boston area. He doesn't have a lot of money, I don't think, so he would probably have to move in with someone."

"So you want me to find where Ronald went with Ed?"

"Yes." Her tone became determined. "And I

want you to get him back for me."

"I understand your feelings. I think we can probably find him fairly quickly. As for the rest of it, I don't know. Give all the information you have, and I'll do the first step, and think about the second."

"Please. Whatever you can do. I don't know what I will do without Ed." Her face was flushed the color of the flowers on her dress and the desperation shown through her eyes.

I took out my pad and took as much information as Natalie had to give. I told her I would get right to the locate and get back to her. As I headed out the front door, the lady of the house stood in the back of the hallway, watching me leave, icy hot.

Back in my office, I ran some locates on the runaway Ronald and found he indeed had some relatives in the area. The most promising was a widowed mother, living on the north shore. It would make sense to take little Ed to Grannies. She was in Marblehead, a coastal community with a monopoly on charm, about thirty miles north of the city. I sent Helen, an enthusiastic field investigator to drive up there to scope it out. It only took an hour to get her excited phone call.

"Bingo," she said. "I go by the house and what do I see? A car with Maryland plates on it. As you trained me well, I consider that a clue."

"You've obviously learned from the great wizard. What else?

"So, I parked up the street, and walked around to the back of the house. And what do I see? Another clue."

"I'm waiting anxiously."

"A little boy sitting in the back yard, all by himself. He was pushing around some building blocks, sitting on the grass."

"OK, we'll check the plate to make sure, but what are the odds against? Good job."

I called Natalie to let her know what we had found. The phone was answered by a voice that suggested promises of exotic pleasures, ending tragically, obviously the lady of the house.

'Hi, Dan Hughes, is Natalie there?"

No response, but dead air and, after a minute, Natalie came on."

"Hi, Natalie. We found Ronald and apparently Ed. They are apparently at his mother's in Marblehead. You can probably go up there and have a chat with him as to the custody protocols."

Her voice was shaky and high pitched. "I can't do that. He'll just lie to me and take off again. I think you have to go up there and get Ed for me."

"I really don't do that." I could hear her quietly sobbing on the line.

"Please, Mr. Hughes. I can't live without Ed and Ronald is impossible. He's a sneaky liar and will push me around." I had a feeling Ronald had done a lot of pushing on Natalie in the past. I was weakening. I was quiet for a minute, and then gave in. "OK, Natalie, let me go and take a look and see what I can do."

The next morning, after I called Natalie again and found that nothing had changed, I took a ride up the coast. The house was a large box colonial with peeling

Yankee yellow paint and a tangle of beach roses in the front yard. It sat on a street with similar houses, mostly throwbacks to the days of the whalers and gentler times. I parked a block away and casually sauntered up the street, trying not to look like a private eye. I felt like a priest walking through a Victoria Secrets store.

The car was parked in a short driveway on the left. We had run the plates and, indeed, Ronald had made his way back to Mom's. Not deeply in hiding. The good news was the house was on a corner, with a mostly dirt road running down the right side, to the next block. The back yard was surrounded by an aging stockade fence, with enough broken and cracked slats to give peeky views into the area. No sign of little Ed, or the sneaky Ronald, but Sesame Street could have been on television at the time. There was a back gate with a drop down inside latch. I figured it could easily be shimmed from the outside. It was doable.

Back at the office, I gathered Helen and Hector with me and worked out a plan. I would shim the gate and grab little Ed. Hector would be behind me to run interference, while Helen sat in the car up on the corner, keeping out of sight. If I was successful, and Hector wasn't needed to throw his substantial body into the fray, we'd signal Helen to speed to us. Hector would take over the wheel, while I passed the terrified Ed to Helen for maternal comforting.

I would walk smartly away to my car, parked up the street. Sacrificing me if Ronald was bright enough to realize what was happening. If he was, my job was to delay until Hector and Helen were outside the town limits. In the meantime, Natalie had a chartered flight standing by a Logan to fly the hapless little Ed back to his proper home. When I finished, Hector made some whispered comment about the three stooges.

I dispatched Helen back to the house for the next three days to see if there was a pattern for Ed's backyard playtime. There was. About 11 A.M., he played in back, sometimes with Granny overseeing, sometimes apparently alone, but watched from the house. It rained the next day and we waited another day, and then with Helen behind the wheel, she and Hector drove in her car while I followed in mine the thirty miles north on a pristinely perfect summer day. As we drove up the coast, the sea was flat, sunshine sparkling off the surface like Christmas tree lights. White and grey gulls glided effortlessly over the mostly empty beaches, and the air was heavy with summer.

The neighborhood was quiet, with only an elderly dog walker two blocks away. I parked a quarter of a mile away from the house and jumped in with Helen and Hector. We circled twice and saw no activity around the house, although Ronald's car was in the driveway. The narrow dirt road along side the house was dimly shaded with leafy Maples and the gate, halfway down was closed. I had Helen stop a half block away and sit tight with Hector slouched down in the back seat, while I strolled down in front of the house and turned down the side road. I couldn't have felt more conspicuous if I was wearing a clown outfit and carrying a brace of balloons. As I walked past the gate in the fence, I was able to peer through the cracks into the back yard of the old colonial. There he was, little Ed sitting in a sand box, with no watcher in sight. I quickened my pace as much as possible without looking like I was fleeing a bank robbery and moved around the block to where Helen and Hector were discussing the rules of sexual harassment. Slightly out of breath, I got to the car and whispered through the half opened driver's window, "It's a go. Helen, move the car to the top of the dirt road, leave the car running and get into the back seat and wait to receive the merchandise. Hector; give me a twenty yard head start on come on behind me. I'm going to try to snatch the kid and pass him to you. Get him into the back seat and get the fuck out of here. Call Natalie and have her standing by. You know the plan."

    I started walking back. I heard Helen start the car and knew Hector was lopping along behind me. I turned down the dirt road, listening for anything, but only heard birds chirping in riotous disarray and distant traffic noise. My heart was pumping like a jack hammer. As I walked down the road, I reached into my pocket and pulled out a four inch shim. When I got to the gate, I stopped and peeked inside. Out of the corner of my eye, I saw Helen stop the car at the top of the drive, Hector standing between me and her, and little Ed, still sitting alone. The gate was latched from inside and I ran the shim up and popped it off. With a last minute adrenaline rush, I pushed the gate open, took two steps inside and picked up Ed. His eyes opened as wide a saucers and he smiled. Holding him close to me, I sprinted the thirty feet to Hector and handed him over. That's when he started crying. Hector passed him to Helen in the back seat, jumped behind the wheel and was around the corner in and gone immediately. I stood in the side road for a minute to see if anyone came rushing out. When no one did, I walked to the front of the house and rang the doorbell. A granny smith type opened the door with a smile and said,

"Yes?"

I said, "Tell Ronald that Ed has gone back to Natalie." I then stood there while she computed my words. Ronald must have been close by, because he came running out red with rage, and fists clenched. He charged towards me, and stopped just short of charging into me, spittle flying and eyes wild.

"You fucker," he screamed, "Where's my son?" Then, before I could answer, he yelled, "Mom, call 911."

I tried to be calm, working against the fight or flee urge. "Ronald, Ed has gone back to his mom. You'll have to talk to her."

He was apoplectic, his anger spilling out like a waterfall. I could tell he wanted to attack me, but was afraid to do so. He stood threatening, shaking all over. The first cruiser thankfully arrived within minutes. Two pots bellied and slightly disheveled cops jumped out, hands on their holstered sidearms and waddled to us. Ronald turned and screamed, "He kidnapped my son," pointing at me with a trembling finger. I held my hands out and up and "Officers, the boy's mother has taken him back after an illegal custody abuse." This confused them. But, Ronald kept screaming unintelligibly at them, and they figured out I was the bad guy. Hands up, they patted me down and cuffed me, pushing my head down and into the cruiser. By that time, another officer pulled up and took Ronald in his. We went the five minutes to the police station where I was pushed into an interrogation room, while Ronald continued to hyperventilate outside. A detective and the Chief came into the room stood over me menacingly. I had a letter from Natalie's attorney, explaining the domestic situation. No formal custody at the time Ronald spirited little Ed out of Baltimore, but a petition for full custody for the mother pending, with possession nine tenths of the law; possession now with Natalie.

They glared at me like I was a festering mold and told me to sit tight until they made some calls. I could hear Ronald continuing his rant.

Thirty uncomfortable minutes later, the Chief came back and stood by the door with his hands on his hips. "You're a sleazy scumbag, but council says you're legal. Get the fuck out of here and don't ever come back to my town."

I said, "Thank you Chief. This is one of those things that, no matter how right it is, it feels wrong. The boy is back where he should be, but I still feel for the father. Never should have taken him in the first place."

His glare softened and he nodded and stepped aside as I made my way out. Ronald was still there, flushed with still clenched fists.

"Sorry, man, but you didn't do it the right way." I said to him as I left.

"You son of a bitch."

I got back to my car and headed out of town as

fast as I could legally. I figured I would be stopped for some imagined driving violation, but crossed the town line clear.

Hector, Helen and little Ed, made it safely to Logan, where Natalie had a Lear Jet standing by. Helen managed to coo little Ed into a slight degree of calm and he perked up happily when he saw his mom.

Four hours later, I got a call from Natalie. Little Ed's grandparents meet them when the plane landed and a joyous reunion occurred, even though little Ed was more concerned with the bag of toys he got during the flight. Natalie sounded like a groupie meeting a rock star backstage. "Dan, I can't thank you enough. You were wonderful and saved us."

"Natalie, I'm glad it worked out for you, but it's too bad it had to happen."

Her voice hardened, "If it wasn't for Ronald, none of this would have been necessary. He'll pay for stealing Ed from me."

"Well, I hope you don't need me again." I said.

"I'll stay in touch if your professional services are needed. Also your non-professional services. Come to visit us in Baltimore. Little Ed would like to thank his savior. When we first met, and I saw your gun, I knew you would save us." I didn't know what gun she was talking about."

"I'll see how my schedule looks," I lied. "Give little Ed a hug for me." It was hard to get her off the phone, but I needed the break away from it all and finally did.

Two weeks later she let me know that the custody hearing went very well for her and that Ronald screamed and ranted all through the hearings. For the next ten years, on my birthday, I large bouquet of flowers showed up from Natalie and she kept inviting me to Baltimore, or New York when she was there. I never did figure out how she knew my birthday and avoided the temptation.

Never again.

Epilogue

All of these stories are true. Of course, names have been changed, but I imagine some of the principles can figure out who is who.

These are only a few of the many cases I've handled in more than thirty years. I've chosen some that hopefully are fun to read, as most are simply identifying the thief, getting a confession and either moving for criminal prosecution, getting restitution or simply throwing him/her out the door of their employment. There are literary thousands of these. After a while, routine.

Being a private investigator these days is like any other profession, moving daily into more and more high tech, working with clients and keeping a sense of humor. The sleaziness once associated is wearing off as the need grows in our increasingly complicated world. But along the way, I've had a lot of fun and, like my mentor Erwin, will never quit.

Made in the USA
Charleston, SC
06 June 2011